BORN WILD:
KODA'S ODYSSEY

VOL. 1

BRIAN KING-SHARP

HANGAR 1 PUBLISHING

GENESIS

S pring had always been a time of renewal in the Olympic Peninsula, but this year, the air felt different. Asha could sense it, a subtle but undeniable shift that pulsed through the forest like a slow, creeping shadow. The season's arrival wasn't marked by just the usual signs—the thawing earth, budding trees, and the nighttime chorus of frogs. This was something more profound, a weight that hung on the wind and wove through the underbrush. It sent shivers down her spine and heightened every sense, as if the world itself was holding its breath. She felt it in her bones, as surely as the new life growing inside her. Asha, with her thick, tawny hair and wise, silver-flecked eyes, had experienced many springs in her life, but none had ever carried such weight. This season, she would bring her child into the world. She had known for some time now, from the way her belly had grown heavy and Kabota had begun watching her with that protective, anxious look in his eyes. Her mate, strong and silent as always, had grown restless, constantly scanning the horizon for any sign of danger.

But the danger wasn't just the rogue sasquatch that roamed the northern ridges—though he posed a threat, to be sure. It was the humans. They grew closer, encroaching on their home, their forest, with each passing day.

Kabota stood at the edge of the clearing, his broad shoulders tense as he listened to the distant machines—human machines. His hair, the color of rich, forest soil, seemed to blend seamlessly with the surrounding trees. From afar, he could have passed for one of the towering ancient cedars, a figure carved from the wilderness itself. But up close, Asha caught the truth—his eyes burned with tension, and his muscles coiled beneath his thick, untamed hair, vibrating with a raw, restless energy that betrayed his unease. "They're getting bolder," he mumbled, his voice low and gravelly. "I saw their fires last night, closer than they've ever been. We may not have much time before they find us."

Asha sat beside him, her hand resting on her swollen belly, feeling the life stir within. "We'll find a way," she said softly, though uncertainty weighed on her heart. "We always do."

But even as she said the words, she wasn't sure she believed them. The humans were relentless. They came in greater numbers each year, pushing deeper into the forest with their strange tools and loud machines, tearing down trees that had stood for centuries. They were careless, trampling the land as if it were theirs to claim. Asha had seen them up close once, years ago, when she had ventured too close to one of their camps. Though smaller than her kind, something terrified her about their numbers and the strange, hard objects they carried—tools that could rip through the forest with ease, as though nature itself bent to their will.

"They're close," Kabota continued, his eyes narrowing as he sniffed the air. "Too close."

Asha followed his gaze to the horizon, where the trees thinned out into open land. She could almost smell the smoke from the human fires, the acrid scent of burning wood mixing with the sweet fragrance of pine needles and moss. That smell always made her uneasy. The humans didn't belong here. They didn't respect the land the way her kind did. They took and took, never giving anything back.

"They won't stop," she said, almost to herself. "Not until they've taken everything."

Kabota growled low in his throat, a sound of frustration and helplessness. "Then we need to prepare."

Asha knew he was right. With the humans closing in and the baby's birth approaching, they needed to find a safe place, a hidden place where she could bring their child into the world without fear of discovery. It wasn't just a matter of comfort—it was survival. The humans were a threat, but so was the forest itself. Dangers for a newborn filled the world, from predators that stalked in the underbrush to weather that could turn from drizzle to torrential storms within hours.

After days of searching the forest, venturing ever deeper into the heart of their territory in search of a safe haven. At last, they found it —a secluded grove, tucked away within a dense stand of ancient cedars, offering the shelter they desperately needed. The trunks of the massive trees stretched wide enough to hide a family of sasquatches from view, their branches forming a dense canopy that shielded the ground from the harsh elements. Scents of pine and damp earth thickened the air, and a nearby stream trickled through the silence, offering both fresh water and a natural barrier between them and any approaching danger.

"This will do," Kabota said, his voice thick with determination.

The two got straight to work, gathering materials for a nest to cradle Asha and their unborn child. Asha's movements had slowed, the weight of the pregnancy making every step more laborious, but she refused to let Kabota do all the work. She wove together long, flexible branches, creating a sturdy foundation, while Kabota gathered piles of soft moss and leaves to line the inside. They worked side by side, as always, their hands moving in rhythm with the forest around them.

Asha took her time selecting the softest moss, pressing it into the base of the nest until it formed a thick, cushiony bed. It needed to be perfect—strong enough to support her weight during the birth, but soft enough to protect the delicate form of their child when the time came. Kabota used his powerful arms to gather animal hides they had saved from past hunts, draping them over the nest to provide warmth and shelter from the cool spring nights.

As they worked, Asha felt a flutter in her belly, a reminder of the life growing inside her. The baby was strong—she could feel it in the way he kicked and shifted, already testing his strength against the confines of her body. A smile tugged at her lips despite the exhaustion. This child would be special.

"It's almost ready," Kabota said, standing back to admire their work. "Just a few more branches to cover the top."

Asha nodded, her hand resting on her belly. "We'll be safe here," she said softly. "At least for a while."

But even as she spoke the words, she couldn't shake the feeling that safety was fleeting. The humans were relentless, always pushing forward, always expanding. And the other danger—the one that stalked the shadows of their territory.

No one ever spoke his name aloud, but everyone knew who he was. The rogue sasquatch. A giant among giants, even larger than Kabota, with a temper as wild as the storms that swept through the mountains. He had no clan, no family; he lived alone, a creature of pure instinct and rage. The stories about him were dark and terrifying, passed down from parents, whispered in the darkness by the older sasquatch who had seen him and survived.

Legends said the rogue had once been in a clan, long ago, but was cast out for reasons no one could fully explain. Some said he had killed his own kin in a fit of rage. Others claimed he had simply grown too wild, too dangerous, even for his own kind. Most believed he had killed many hikers on the Appalachian Trail who dared to venture too far into the backcountry near his old clan's territory. Whatever the truth, he was an unsettling presence—a relentless threat woven into the fabric of the forest, unseen yet impossible to ignore, pressing at the periphery of awareness like the weight of an impending storm. Asha had never seen him herself, but Kabota had. Once, many years ago, before they had become mates. He didn't talk about it much, but she knew the encounter had left a deep impression on him.

"I saw him near the northern ridge," Kabota had told her one night by the fire. His voice had been low, almost a whisper, as if speaking of the rogue would summon him from the shadows. "He was huge. Bigger than any of us. His hair was dark, almost black, and his eyes... They were wild. Like nothing I've ever seen. He wasn't like us, Asha. He was ... something else."

Asha had shivered at the memory of Kabota's words. They could not ignore the danger of the rogue, especially now with the baby on the way. They would need to stay alert, always on guard, in case he wandered too close to their territory.

But for now, they focused on the nest. On the birth.

PART I

1

BIRTH

Asha went into labor on a calm, clear night. The sky above the canopy was a deep, velvety black, dotted with stars that twinkled faintly through the gaps in the trees. The air, cool but not cold. It should have been a peaceful night, a night for resting and gathering strength. Instead, pain wracked Asha's body. It started slowly, a dull ache deep in her belly that made her shift uncomfortably in the nest. Kabota stood beside her, his large frame casting a protective shadow over the entrance to their shelter. He had been restless all day, sensing the time was near, and now that it had come, his eyes were sharp with concern.

"Asha?" His voice was gentle but had an edge to it, a quiet urgency. "Is it time?"

Asha nodded, unable to speak as another wave of pain rolled through her. She gripped the edge of the nest, her breath coming in short, sharp gasps. The baby was coming. She could feel it, the pressure building inside her, her body instinctively preparing for the birth.

Kabota knelt beside her, his hand resting on her shoulder, offering her what comfort he could. "I'm here. I'm not going anywhere."

The hours that followed were a blur of pain and effort, her body straining with the intensity of the labor. Each contraction seemed to tear through her like fire, but Asha remained focused, her mind fixed on the life she was about to bring into the world. She could feel the baby moving inside her, shifting lower, ready to emerge. Kabota stayed by her side the entire time, his presence a steady, grounding force as she fought through the pain. He wiped the sweat from her brow with a cool clump of moss, his deep voice whispering words of encouragement as the night dragged on.

"You're strong, Asha," he whispered. "You can do this. You're almost there."

Finally, after what felt like an eternity, the baby came. With one last, agonizing push, Asha felt the release of pressure as the child slid from her body into the world. The first sound to fill the air was a tiny, sharp cry—a cry that sent a wave of relief and joy through her, even as her body trembled with exhaustion. Kabota caught the newborn in his large hands, his face filled with awe and wonder as he looked down at their son.

He was small, covered in soft, dark hair, his eyes wide and blinking as he took in his first breaths of the world outside the womb.

"Koda," Asha whispered, her voice barely a breath. She reached out, and Kabota gently placed the baby in her arms, his tiny form warm and alive against her chest. "Our son." Asha gazed down at him, her heart swelling with love and pride. He was perfect, their Koda, their strong and beautiful boy. But as she held him close, she felt another sharp pain rip through her body—unexpected, and wrong.

A second baby.

Asha gasped, her eyes widening in shock as her body convulsed again. Kabota's face twisted with concern as he realized what was happening. A twin. They hadn't known. But as the second baby came into the world, Asha immediately knew something was wrong.

There was no cry.

Kabota's face fell as he gently lifted the still, silent form of their daughter. She was small, too small, her body limp and lifeless in his hands. Asha's heart shattered as she reached out to touch her daughter's tiny face, tears spilling down her cheeks.

"Kabota..." Her voice broke, thick with grief.

Kabota didn't speak. He couldn't. His face was a mask of sorrow as he wrapped their daughter in soft leaves, his hands trembling as he prepared her for burial. Asha watched through a veil of tears as he carried her out of the nest, into the grove where the ancient cedar trees stood like silent sentinels.

They buried their daughter beneath the largest tree, the earth cool and damp as Kabota gently laid her to rest. Asha knelt beside the grave, her heart heavy with loss. They had gained a son, but they had lost a daughter. The joy and sorrow mingled in a way that left Asha hollow, like a piece of her soul had been torn away.

"We will never forget you, Katia," she whispered, her hand resting on the freshly turned soil. "You will always be with us."

The days after the birth were a blur of exhaustion and quiet mourning. Asha and Kabota took turns watching over Koda, their grief for their daughter lingering like a shadow over their small family. But even in their sorrow, they knew they had to stay vigilant. The humans were getting closer, and the rogue still lurked somewhere in the forest.

Each day, the sounds of human activity grew louder—machines tearing through the earth, the distant roar of engines, and the sharp crack of trees being felled. The once quiet forest was now filled with the noise of human expansion, and it was only a matter of time before they stumbled upon Asha and Kabota's nest.

"They're coming," Kabota said one evening, his voice heavy with resignation. "We need to move."

Asha nodded, holding Koda close as he slept. They couldn't stay here any longer. The humans were relentless, and with a newborn to protect, they couldn't afford to take any chances.

But more than just the humans worried Asha. The rogue sasquatch was still out there, somewhere in the shadows, a threat looming over them like a dark cloud. She had seen signs of him—

broken branches, disturbed earth, and the unmistakable stench of his presence. He was close. Too close.

"We'll find a new place," Asha said, though her voice lacked confidence. "Somewhere deeper in the forest."

Kabota nodded, worry etched clearly in his eyes. The forest, once their sanctuary, no longer offered safety. The humans advanced steadily, and the rogue posed a threat they couldn't afford to overlook.

With heavy hearts, they left the grove behind, carrying Koda in their arms as they ventured deeper into the wilderness. The forest stretched out before them, vast and untamed, full of both danger and promise.

But Asha knew one thing for certain: they would do whatever it took to protect their family. They had survived the loss of their daughter, the encroachment of humans, and the impending threat of the rogue. They would survive whatever came next. They had to.

2

GROWTH

It had been a few days since Asha had given birth to little Koda. Her newborn was nursing well, and Asha was recovering quickly. But the human presence was getting closer and closer to their nest, forcing Asha and Kabota to make some tough decisions.

"We can't stay here anymore," Kabota said grimly one evening. "The humans are getting too close. We need to move deeper into the forest, find a new place to make our home."

Asha nodded solemnly, casting a worried glance down at the sleeping Koda. "I was afraid of this. But you're right, we can't risk them finding us here. It's not safe for Koda."

Kabota reached out and caressed Koda's soft hair. "Don't worry, we'll find a good place to go. Somewhere the humans won't be able to get to us." He paused. "We'll have to leave first thing in the morning."

Asha sighed heavily. "All right. I'll start getting ready. This was such a good home for us..."

Kabota pulled her into a comforting embrace. "I know. But we'll find another. And Koda will be safe. That's what matters most."

The next morning, they set out with Koda snuggled securely against Asha's chest. Kabota led them deeper into the dense forest, keeping a watchful eye for any sign of the humans. After a few hours of trekking, they came across a small clearing that seemed like a good spot to set up a new temporary home.

"This looks promising," Kabota said, surveying the area. "Lots of cover, away from any trails the humans might use. We can build a shelter here and hunker down for a while."

Asha nodded in agreement, rocking Koda as he fussed. "All right, let's get started then. The sooner we get settled, the better I'll feel."

They worked quickly to construct a simple lean-to structure using branches, leaves, and whatever they found in the clearing. Though not the most sturdy or weatherproof shelter, it would have to do for now. As the sun set, they huddled inside, Koda nestled warmly between them.

"There, that should do it," Kabota said, giving the structure a pat. "It's not much, but it'll keep the rain off at least."

Asha nodded, running a hand over Koda's soft hair. "It's perfect. I just hope it keeps us hidden from the humans."

Kabota drew closer, wrapping a comforting arm around her. "Don't worry, we're well off the trails now. I don't think they'll find us here."

They settled in for the night, Koda snoozing peacefully while Asha and Kabota kept watch. But as they drifted off, a sudden, bone-chilling howl pierced the silence of the forest.

Asha stiffened, eyes going wide. "What was that?"

Kabota tensed, listening intently. "I don't know, but it didn't sound good." He paused, then let out a series of low, rumbling grunts—a warning call to any threats in the area.

They waited, straining their ears for any other sounds. After a few tense moments, another howl echoed through the trees, closer this time. Kabota responded with more grunts, deeper and more insistent.

Asha huddled closer to Koda, heart pounding. "Kabota, what is it? What's out there?"

"I'm not sure, but whatever it is, it's getting closer. Stay close to me, and keep quiet."

They fell silent, listening as the forest seemed to come alive around them. Twigs snapped, leaves rustled, and a strange, guttural growling reached their ears. Kabota's grunts grew louder, more desperate, as he tried to ward off the unseen threat.

Suddenly, a towering, shadowy figure loomed at the edge of their little shelter. Asha stifled a gasp, clutching Koda. Kabota rose to his feet, letting out a series of deep, booming barks—a clear warning for the intruder to back off.

The figure paused, then let out a bone-chilling scream that made Asha's blood run cold. It was a primal, animalistic sound, full of raw power and aggression. Kabota responded with a series of thunderous mouth pops, like a bat striking a tree, hoping to intimidate the larger sasquatch.

For a moment, the two giants stared each other down. Then, with a final, earth-shaking roar, the figure retreated back into the darkness of the forest.

Asha let out a shaky breath, heart racing. "Kabota, what was that?"

Kabota remained tense, eyes scanning the tree line. "I think... I think it was the rogue. The one we've been hearing about." For the first time, he spoke his name. "Adanowa, the Cherokee word for war."

Asha's eyes widened in fear. "Adanowa? But why would he come so close to our shelter? He's never done that before."

Kabota shook his head slowly. "I don't know, but I'm sure it has something to do with Koda. Either way, we need to be careful from now on. He's dangerous, and he's not afraid to come after us." They huddled in the small shelter, Koda whimpering softly in Asha's arms. The rest of the night passed in tense silence, with both Asha and Kabota keeping vigil, alert for any sign of the rogue's return.

As the first rays of dawn filtered through the trees, Kabota finally relaxed a bit, letting out a heavy sigh. "I think it's gone for now, but we need to find a more secure place to stay, something that can better protect us."

Asha nodded, rocking Koda. "Agreed. The sooner we can get moved, the better. I don't want to risk Koda's safety."

They quickly packed up what little they had and set out, Kabota leading the way deeper into the forest. The going was slow, with Asha having to carry Koda and Kabota constantly on the lookout for any sign of Adanowa. After several hours of trekking, they came across a small cave, partially hidden by a tangle of fallen trees and overgrown vegetation. Kabota paused, studying it closely.

"This could work." He ran a hand along the rough stone. "It's secluded, and the entrance is well-hidden. We should be able to fortify it and make it a decent shelter." Asha peered inside, Koda still cradled against her chest. "It does seem promising. And if that rogue comes back, at least we'll have some protection."

Kabota nodded. "Exactly. Let's get started. Tthe sooner we get settled, the better I'll feel."

They spent the rest of the day working to clear out the cave and reinforce the entrance. Kabota gathered large branches and sturdy logs to create a makeshift barricade, while Asha gathered soft bedding materials and arranged a cozy nest for Koda. By nightfall, they had a relatively secure and comfortable shelter to call home.

As they settled in for the evening, Kabota kept an eye on the forest around them. "I haven't heard any sign of Adanowa since last night. Hopefully he's moved on."

Asha nodded, gently stroking Koda's hair. "Let's hope so. I don't think I could handle another confrontation like that."

Kabota reached out and squeezed her hand. "Don't worry, I won't let anything happen to you or Koda. I'll keep us safe. I promise." They fell into a light sleep, Kabota waking periodically to check the perimeter. But just as the first hints of dawn peeked over the horizon, a howl shattered the stillness of the forest.

3

TENSION

Kabota's eyes snapped open, and he bolted upright, a low, rumbling growl building in his chest. Asha sat up as well, clutching Koda. "He's back," Kabota whispered, already moving to reinforce the cave's entrance. "Stay inside. Keep quiet."

Asha nodded, her heart pounding in her chest. She huddled deeper into the cave, shielding Koda with her body as Kabota went to work. The howling grew closer, accompanied by the snapping of branches and the rustling of leaves. Kabota braced himself, ready to defend his family at all costs. Suddenly, a massive figure emerged from the trees, towering over the makeshift barricade. Kabota let out a series of thunderous barks, his deep, booming voice echoing through the forest.

Adanowa paused, then unleashed an earth-shaking roar in response. It was a sound that seemed to vibrate through Asha's very bones, and she had to fight the urge to leave the safety of the cave to join Kabota to defend their newfound home.

Kabota answered with more barks, his own voice rising in volume and intensity. The two sasquatches stared each other down, the tension thick enough to cut with a knife. For a moment, it seemed like they might come to blows. But then, Adanowa let out a final, guttural growl and turned, disappearing back into the trees. Kabota waited, listening intently, before finally relaxing his stance. He hurried back to the cave, checking on Asha and Koda.

"Are you both all right?" he asked, his voice tinged with concern.

Asha nodded, still trembling. "Yes, we're fine. But, Kabota, he is so much bigger than you. I'm scared for us, for Koda."

Kabota reached out and pulled her into an embrace. "I know, I know. But I won't let him hurt us. I promise. We're safe here, in this cave. That rogue won't be able to get to us."

Asha buried her face in his chest, taking comfort in his warmth and strength. "I hope you're right. I don't know what I'd do if something happened to you or Koda."

They stayed like that for a while, Kabota gently soothing Asha's fears. Finally, as the sun began to rise, they settled back down, Koda nestled safely between them.

The next few days passed in relative peace, with no sign of the rogue. Kabota used the time to keep fortifying their new home, reinforcing the entrance and gathering supplies.

Asha, meanwhile, focused on caring for Koda and keeping him warm and safe. She was relieved to be in the more secure cave, away from the prying eyes of the humans.

One evening, as they huddled, Kabota turned to Asha, a serious expression on his face.

"Asha, I think we need to start thinking about what we're going to do if that rogue comes back. We can't rely on this cave to protect us forever."

Asha looked up. "What do you mean? Where else could we go?"

Kabota sighed, running a hand through his thick hair. "I'm not sure. But we need to be prepared. He's dangerous, and it's clear he's not going to leave us alone." Asha glanced down at Koda snuggled against her chest, fast asleep. "I don't want to have to move again. Koda is still so young, and I'm worried about exposing him to more danger."

Kabota reached out and gently squeezed her hand. "I know. But we have to do what's best for him, and for all of us. If that rogue comes back, and we can't defend ourselves here, we may have no choice but to keep moving."

Asha nodded slowly, her heart heavy. "All right. I'll think about what to do, where we could go. But, Kabota, promise me you'll do everything you can to keep us safe here."

Kabota met her gaze, his expression resolute. "I promise, Asha. I'll fight him with everything I have if I have to. I won't let him hurt you or Koda, no matter what."

Asha felt hope in the midst of her fear. Kabota was her rock, her protector, and she knew he would do whatever it took to keep their family safe.

4

FIGHT

As the days passed, Asha and Kabota continued to fortify their cave, stockpiling supplies and keeping a constant watch for any sign of the rogue menace. But the relative peace shattered one rainy night, when the unmistakable howl of the rogue echoed through the forest.

Kabota got to his feet in an instant, his body tense and ready to defend. Asha clutched Koda, her heart pounding in her chest. The howling neared, with crashing branches and rumbling growls. Kabota responded with a series of mouth pops, the sound thundering through the cave.

Suddenly, a massive silhouette appeared near the entrance, barely visible through the driving rain. Kabota roared, his voice directed at the threat. Adanowa paused, then unleashed a scream of his own that Asha could feel in her chest. She could see it now, the towering, hulking form of the massive sasquatch.

Kabota made more mouth pops, trying to intimidate the larger creature, to make it back down without a fight. But Adanowa was undeterred. He took a step forward, filling the entrance to the cave. Asha pressed herself and Koda as far back as she could, her emotions a mix anger and terror in equal measure.

Kabota would fight to the death if necessary. He was younger and nimbler than the rogue, but the sheer size and power of the creature was daunting. He'd hoped to drive him off without violence.

Kabota stepped forward, out of the cave and into the open, meeting Adanowa's glare head-on. His heart pounded as he sized up his opponent. Adanowa was larger, older, and scarred from many battles. Dark stains from past conflicts streaked his thick, matted hair, and his eyes glinted with feral determination.

Kabota stood his ground, puffing up his chest, resonating a deep growl throughout the clearing. He began the mouth pops and guttural sounds meant to warn intruders, signaling his claim to the territory, but Adanowa seemed unfazed, his expression unmoved, his stance steady as he took another step forward. Kabota felt the weight of the rogue's gaze, a silent but potent threat.

With a roar, Adanowa charged, his massive form shaking the ground with every step. Kabota braced himself, muscles coiled like springs, as the rogue thundered forward. The gap between them vanished in an instant. Kabota twisted at the last second, narrowly dodging the powerful swipe of Adanowa's arm, but the rogue's momentum clipped him. The impact was like a battering ram, sending him skidding backward.

Kabota grunted, the pain sharp and immediate, but he steadied himself. His chest heaved as he locked eyes with Adanowa, who growled low, baring jagged teeth. The rogue didn't wait—he lunged again, relentless. Kabota surged forward to meet him, his fist driving into Adanowa's ribs with a dull thud. The rogue grunted but barely faltered, retaliating with a backhanded strike that sent Kabota sprawling to the ground.

Rolling with the blow, Kabota scrambled to his feet, his vision swimming. He shook his head, forcing the dizziness aside, and focused on Adanowa's advancing form. Each step was deliberate, heavy, brimming with menace. Kabota's mind raced. He couldn't match Adanowa's brute strength—he had to be faster, sharper.

When Adanowa's massive arm rose for another strike, Kabota feigned retreat, luring the rogue closer. At the last moment, he ducked low and surged forward, tackling Adanowa's waist. The impact drove them both to the ground with a thunderous crash. Kabota clung to the rogue, delivering rapid, calculated punches to his ribcage. Adanowa roared, thrashing violently, his claws slicing deep into Kabota's side. Warm blood trickled down Kabota's ribs, but he gritted his teeth and held on.

Adanowa twisted with terrifying strength, throwing Kabota off like a ragdoll. Both scrambled to their feet, battered and bloodied. Kabota's side throbbed, the pain pulling at the edges of his focus, but he forced it down. He couldn't afford to falter—not now.

The rogue let out another deafening roar and charged again. Kabota sidestepped, his claws catching Adanowa's arm. With a sharp twist, he wrenched it behind the rogue's back. A sickening pop echoed as the joint strained under Kabota's grip. Adanowa howled, but before Kabota could press his advantage, the rogue's free arm swung like a sledgehammer, slamming into Kabota's jaw. Kabota stumbled, the world spinning. His knees buckled, and for a fleeting moment, darkness threatened to overtake him. But he fought through it, shaking his head to clear his vision. Adanowa loomed above him, his fiery gaze promising death. Kabota barely dodged the next strike, the rogue's fist grazing his shoulder as it crashed into the ground with enough force to send dirt flying.

Breathing hard, Kabota noted the hitch in Adanowa's step—a slight limp. The rogue was wearing down. Summoning what strength he had left, Kabota faked left, then darted right, his foot connecting hard with Adanowa's injured leg. The rogue stumbled, his balance wavering. Kabota lunged, claws raking across Adanowa's face. Blood streaked down the rogue's cheek as he roared in pain, but Kabota pressed on.

He drove his fist into Adanowa's abdomen, the blow forcing the air from the rogue's lungs. As Adanowa doubled over, Kabota gripped his arm and twisted with all his might. The bone snapped with a sharp, gut-turning crack, and Adanowa's howl of agony echoed through the forest.

For a moment, Kabota thought it was over. Adanowa sagged, blood dripping from countless wounds, his breaths ragged and shallow. But desperation fueled the rogue. With a final, enraged snarl, he lashed out with his uninjured arm. Kabota couldn't dodge in time. The rogue's claws tore across his chest, leaving deep, jagged gashes. Kabota staggered, clutching the wound as warm blood seeped between his fingers. His strength was nearly gone, his body battered and raw, but he refused to fall.

Standing tall, Kabota growled low and steady, a primal warning that echoed in the tense silence. Adanowa hesitated, trembling from exhaustion and pain, his body quivering with the effort to stay upright. Finally, with a defeated snarl, the rogue turned and limped away, his massive form retreating into the shadowy depths of the forest. Kabota watched him disappear, his own body swaying with fatigue. Relief washed over him as the rogue's silhouette vanished, the sound of labored breathing fading into silence. The fight was over- for now.

Kabota stood there a moment, chest heaving, aching. He felt the sting of his injuries, blood trickling down his hair, but he was alive. More importantly, his family was safe.

With a final, weary glance at the forest, Kabota turned and made his way back to the cave, his steps slow and heavy, each a reminder of the cost of the battle he had just won.

Kabota staggered back into the cave, his broad shoulders heaving with every labored breath. He dropped to his knees, trying to slow his heart rate. Asha and Koda watched him, their eyes wide with concern. His thick hair was matted with streaks of dark blood, some of it his own, some of it Adanowa's.

Kabota's right shoulder had taken a beating, and his left forearm bore deep gashes. Pain jolted through his body with every step, but his gaze softened when he saw Asha and Koda. His family, safe. That was all that mattered. Asha took a tentative step forward, reaching out to touch the deep scratch along his ribcage.

"You're hurt," she whispered.

Kabota grunted in response, nodding slowly. "It'll heal, in time," he said. But he knew the bruising and torn flesh would take days, weeks, or maybe months to fully mend. For now, he just wanted to rest. He needed to be at his best if Adanowa returned, though something in him doubted the old rogue would dare to.

5

RECOVERY

Kabota spent the weeks that followed recovering in the cave, his wounds scabbing over as he regained his strength. Asha stayed close, tending to him and Koda, and occasionally leaving to search for berries, fish, and edible roots. They would eventually need to hunt larger prey, but for now, Kabota was grateful to have Asha at his side.

One evening, Kabota stretched out his stiff limbs. The scabs had tightened over his wounds, tugging at his skin, but the pain was becoming bearable. He felt the urge to leave the cave, to move again, even if only to test his strength. He looked at Asha, who had sensed his restlessness, and she gave a slight nod, as if to say, "I'm with you."

"We'll go together," he said, his voice softened with gratitude. "The three of us."

Asha smiled and eased Koda onto her back. The little one clung to her hair, his tiny hands gripping with surprising strength as he nestled between her shoulder blades. They set off into the forest, Kabota moving cautiously, not wanting to overextend himself, while Asha stayed close, occasionally glancing over her shoulder to ensure Kabota was keeping up.

As they ventured deeper into the forest, Kabota scanned the

surroundings, mentally marking signs of animal trails, listening for any distant noises that might betray the presence of deer. The quiet rustling of leaves and the occasional birdsong calmed him, grounding him after the chaos of the recent fight. The scent of deer eventually reached his nostrils, and he motioned for Asha to follow as he led them to a small clearing where he had noticed deer tracks before.

Kabota and Asha worked together, setting up a simple trap that used the natural layout of the forest. They found a narrow area bordered by a fallen log and thick underbrush, perfect for funneling any passing deer into a confined space. Kabota then circled wide around the clearing, using his presence to subtly drive the deer toward Asha. She moved in stealthily, positioning herself along the trap's edge.

Soon, a small deer trotted into the confined space, startled by the sudden presence of the massive creatures. Kabota lunged, his powerful arms encircling the deer's neck, and in one swift motion, he twisted, breaking its neck quickly to minimize its suffering. It was a clean catch, and the family would eat well that night.

They hauled their prize back to the cave, Koda babbling in delight at the feast. Asha looked at Kabota, her eyes filled with pride.

"You're healing well," she said softly. "And still as strong as ever."

Kabota chuckled, though he winced as he laughed. "With you and Koda here, I have no choice but to be strong."

Days passed, and the forest returned to its familiar rhythm. Kabota's wounds continued to heal, and the nights felt peaceful once more. He heard the distant cries of Adanowa less frequently now; thought still out there, the old sasquatch posed no immediate threat. Life, it seemed, was returning to normal, or as close to it as possible in the wild forest.

But one morning, Kabota picked up a scent that tensed his muscles. Faint but unmistakable—the smell of humans. He gestured to Asha, who, sensing his unease, quieted Koda. Together, they crept to the edge of the forest, where they saw faint shadows moving between the trees in the distance. Unlike the loggers who had disturbed them in the past, these humans moved more deliberately, and without the usual machinery.

A distant, rhythmic thudding echoed through the trees. Kabota's eyes narrowed as he tried to make sense of the strange noise. The humans seemed to be hitting trees with some sort of club, mimicking the mouth pops that he and other sasquatches used for communication and territory marking. The sound, though clumsy, set Kabota's nerves on edge.

"These humans... They're looking for us," Asha whispered, barely audible.

Kabota nodded grimly, signaling for her to stay low. He couldn't understand why these humans would try to imitate their sounds unless they had a purpose. A creeping sense of dread settled over him. If they had come looking for sasquatches specifically, it meant they knew more than Kabota had thought possible—and it could mean trouble for him and his family.

They retreated into the cave, lying low and watching from a safe distance as the humans moved deeper into the forest. For hours, the rhythmic knocking continued, each sound reverberating through the trees. Occasionally, Kabota could hear faint voices among the humans, though he couldn't understand their words. Cautious, they checked behind trees and watched the ground as if tracking something.

Days passed, and though the humans retreated at daybreak, they returned each night, systematically moving through different sections of the forest, their calls and noises filling the air. Kabota's patience thinned, but he knew better than to act rashly. One wrong move could reveal their presence.

Asha, ever the quiet observer, collected leaves and branches to disguise the entrance of their cave. Kabota helped, layering moss and twigs, working together in silence to ensure their home remained hidden. As the days went by, they felt more concealed, though the presence of the humans still weighed on them.

Koda, though still young, seemed to understand the need for silence, mimicking his parents as they stayed close and quiet. Kabota's heart swelled with pride at his son's adaptability, but he worried about what these humans might bring if they ever stumbled upon their hidden family.

One evening, as the humans packed up their gear to leave for the day, Kabota noticed a small group lingering longer than the others. These few seemed particularly intent, shining flashlights into the trees and tying bright orange ribbons to branches, marking the path back to their camp. They must have intended to return to that very spot, maybe to investigate further, or worse, to set a trap.

Kabota knew they couldn't stay hidden forever. Keeping his family safe might mean finding a new hiding place, at least until the humans left for good. But moving now, with Asha and young Koda, would be risky. For now, they would have to remain vigilant, their senses attuned to every sound, every scent, and every movement in the forest.

Though the humans' presence weighed on them, Kabota and Asha resolved to stay close to the cave, only venturing out at dawn and dusk to hunt and gather, always careful to avoid leaving any traces of their existence. Their life had changed, but together, they would adapt, as they always had.

The months passed with the silent tension of a family bound together yet wary of the shadows that lingered at the edges of their world.

6

DECISIONS

Kabota and Asha knew it was only a matter of time before Adanowa returned or, worse, that the humans came back, more determined and organized. They had sheltered, healed, and hunted quietly, always vigilant, but a gnawing sense of vulnerability persisted. Kabota could feel the threats to their family growing.

For days, the two had talked late into the night, huddled in the quiet security of their cave, discussing their options. They could stay, risking confrontation with Adanowa or human encroachment. Or they could venture out, joining a clan they'd seen only a few times over the years but knew well enough to trust. Ultimately, they came to a shared understanding: for Koda's safety and their own peace, they would need the strength and numbers that a larger family could offer.

Kabota and Asha soon decided to reach out to this nearby clan. This other group, which they had often seen traveling the edges of their territory, was likely foraging farther north in the Olympic Peninsula, near the densely wooded hills and hidden valleys that had always provided ample cover and food sources. The Hoh Clan, as they called themselves, was known for their resilience and cohesion, a bonded family that had long adapted to life in the lush forests of the peninsula.

The Hoh Clan was led by two older sasquatches, Omaki and Taron, who had guided their family through many seasons of upheaval and adaptation. The rest of the clan consisted of younger sasquatches: Taron's two grown sons, Erek and Varo, and three juveniles—siblings who had come to live with the Hoh Clan after illness claimed their parents. These young ones, barely old enough to roam far on their own, were named Meika, Raela, and Paka. Together, they formed a tight-knit group that rarely ventured beyond the protection of the elder pair.

It was late afternoon when Kabota and Asha decided to make the journey to the area where they suspected the Hoh Clan would be foraging. They moved with care, carrying Koda on Asha's back, each step purposeful and quiet, conscious that they were approaching the clan's territory and needed to be respectful. The forest was dense, the underbrush soft and thick beneath their feet, muffling their steps. Birds flitted above, darting between branches, and the sun shined through the canopy, and cast dappled light across the forest floor. It was a calming contrast to the days of tension they'd endured.

As they neared the boundary where they had last seen traces of the Hoh Clan, Kabota paused, signaling to Asha. He let out a low, steady rumble, a vocalization that signaled a peaceful approach, one meant to communicate that they came in friendship. They waited, the forest silent except for the rustling leaves, until a shadowed figure finally emerged from behind a towering cedar.

It was Omaki, the clan matriarch, her tall, weathered frame moving with an easy grace that belied her years. Her hair was a mix of deep brown and silver, the markings around her face and chest tinged with the grey that came with age. She surveyed Kabota and Asha with a calm but discerning gaze, assessing their intent in the way only an experienced elder could.

"Greetings, Kabota, Asha." Omaki's voice was low, nearly a whisper, carrying a tone of curiosity. "We've seen you before, at a distance. But now you come closer."

Kabota stepped forward respectfully, lowering his gaze as a sign of deference. "We seek your counsel, Omaki," he replied. "Our family is small, and the times are growing uncertain. We face dangers, both from humans and from... others of our kind. We hoped that, perhaps, we could discuss joining your clan, for the safety of all."

Omaki studied them for a long moment before gesturing for them to follow. "Come. We will speak with Taron and the others."

They followed Omaki through the underbrush to a secluded hollow surrounded by towering ferns and fallen logs, where the rest of the Hoh Clan was gathered. Taron, the clan's patriarch, stood up as they approached. He was a formidable presence, taller than Omaki, with thick, auburn hair and a piercing gaze that spoke of a life shaped by the wild. Though his movements were slower than they had once been, the strength in his stance was unmistakable.

Beside Taron stood his two sons, Erek and Varo. Both had inherited their father's build and presence, though they carried themselves in distinct ways. Erek, the elder of the two, was a broad-shouldered, contemplative sasquatch with a keen eye for observation. He rarely spoke, preferring to let his actions communicate for him. Varo, the younger sibling, was leaner, quicker, and known for his curiosity. His gaze was sharp and constantly shifting, as if he were cataloging every detail of the world around him.

At the edge of the hollow, the three juveniles—Meika, Raela, and Paka—watched Kabota and Asha with wide-eyed curiosity. Meika, the oldest of the trio, had a protective air about her, watching over her younger siblings with a maturity that belied her age. Raela, the middle child was more timid, hiding behind her sister, while Paka, the youngest, couldn't resist inching forward, his small form quivering with barely contained excitement.

After Kabota and Asha explained their circumstances, Taron nodded thoughtfully. "The forest has changed since we were young," he said, his voice a deep rumble. "Humans press farther into these woods each year, and we've encountered others like Adanowa, desperate and dangerous."

Omaki looked at Asha, her gaze softening. "We know the need to protect the young," she said gently, nodding toward Koda, who was peeking over Asha's shoulder with wide, curious eyes.

Kabota met Taron's gaze. "We only ask for safety," he said. "We would do whatever is necessary to contribute. We bring our skills, and we are willing to defend the clan as fiercely as our own family."

Erek, who had kept silent throughout, spoke up, his deep voice measured. "We could benefit from extra eyes and hands," he acknowledged. "Adanowa is a familiar name to us. He was once part of a distant clan to the south, but his temper and aggression drove him into exile. I do not doubt he will return one day."

Varo, ever observant, nodded. "And the humans... They seem to learn more each season. They have grown bolder, finding ways to mimic our sounds, leaving marks in places we once considered safe..." His voice trailed off, and he glanced toward the forest, as if expecting to see a human emerge from the shadows.

The clan conferred among themselves, and after a brief discussion, Omaki turned back to Kabota and Asha. "You may join us," she said with a soft smile. "But know that our way is one of unity and shared responsibility. We protect each other, and we look out for each other's young."

Kabota felt a surge of relief and gratitude. "Thank you," he said earnestly, nodding to each member of the Hoh Clan. He could see the warmth in Asha's expression as well, and Koda, sensing the change in the atmosphere, let out a happy coo.

7

COHESION

Over the next few days, Kabota and Asha settled into their new roles within the Hoh Clan, learning the rhythms of the larger family and contributing where they could. Kabota took on patrol duties with Erek and Varo, scouting the borders of the clan's territory and marking areas to ward off any intruders. Asha, meanwhile, helped Omaki and the juveniles with foraging, sharing her knowledge of hidden food sources and teaching the younger ones how to recognize the subtle signs of safe trails and hiding places.

It didn't take long for the bonds within the new clan to solidify. Kabota quickly found respect for Erek's wisdom and insight, admiring his quiet strength and calm demeanor. Erek was known among the Hoh Clan as a skilled tracker and often led the family on foraging trips, using his keen senses to locate food and steer the clan clear of danger.

Varo, the younger of the two siblings, contrasted Erek's steady nature. Restless and curious, he was often the first to notice any changes in their surroundings. Varo had a knack for spotting trails and following even the faintest traces of an animal or human, a skill he'd been honing since youth. Though cautious and responsible when needed, he often found himself drawn to the edge of the clan's territory, to exploring the unknown.

The juveniles quickly grew attached to Koda, who was fascinated by the trio's energy and playfulness. Meika, with her natural sense of responsibility, often led their games, organizing them into quiet activities that kept them out of trouble. She had been orphaned young, taken in by the Hoh Clan when Taron and Omaki found her and her siblings wandering alone. Meika carried the weight of that past, and it showed in her maturity and protectiveness.

Raela, on the other hand, was quiet and observant, always clinging to her older sister but with a gaze that saw deeper than others realized. She would sit for hours, watching the forest with a quiet intensity, sometimes noticing what the adults missed.

Paka, the youngest, was a bundle of energy, bounding around and often getting into harmless mischief. He looked up to Koda, delighted to have someone even younger than himself, though only slightly, to teach and protect.

As seasons passed, Koda grew from a small, curious child into a lively young sasquatch, comfortable and at home within the Hoh Clan. Each day brought new lessons, new adventures, and, most importantly, new bonds. Surrounded by the protective presence of the clan, Koda felt a sense of belonging that only strengthened as he grew closer to his young companions and gained knowledge from his mentors.

Meika was born to lead, and Koda often fell into step behind her as they roamed the forest in search of berries, exploring the trees, or simply sharing stories. She had a knack for knowing the forest's hidden paths and shortcuts, often leading the others along winding trails and through narrow thickets that only the young could navigate. She carried herself with a quiet dignity, her movements careful and deliberate, and the younger ones followed her lead.

One warm morning, the four youngsters decided to explore the edge of the clan's territory, where they had spotted clusters of sweet huckleberries ripening under the spring sun. Meika led the way, her nose twitching as she sniffed the air, catching the faint aroma of the berries in the distance. Koda and Paka trailed, while Raela hung back, her gaze sweeping their surroundings with the wariness of someone who never let her guard down.

"Koda, did you know that if you eat a handful of these berries, you won't be hungry until sunset?" Meika asked, plucking a handful of huckleberries and popping them into her mouth with a mischievous grin.

Koda chuckled, knowing Meika's playful exaggeration well. Still, he relished every berry, savoring the tangy sweetness as they burst in his mouth. Paka, with his boundless energy, darted from bush to bush, gathering as many as his hands could hold, offering a few to Raela, who quietly accepted them, her gaze still sweeping the forest.

"Look!" Koda pointed to a massive fallen log not far from their path. The log had splintered in places, creating small hollows that were ideal hiding spots for critters. He approached it carefully, aware of the potential dangers but intrigued by the possibility of finding something interesting.

Paka scrambled over to him, eyes wide with excitement. "Think there's anything inside?"

Meika nodded, feigning the wisdom of an elder. "The trick is to move slowly and listen carefully," she advised, a glint of mischief in her eyes. "Otherwise, you might end up with a face full of porcupine quills."

Koda, emboldened by Meika's guidance, leaned close, listening for any signs of life inside the log. He heard the faint rustling of leaves and caught a flash of movement—a chipmunk darting out and scurrying away, chittering in alarm. The youngsters laughed, relieved it wasn't anything more dangerous.

"See?" Meika teased, laughing. "You scared it right out of its home."

Their laughter echoed through the trees, mingling with the birdsongs. These carefree moments in the company of his friends filled Koda with a deep sense of happiness. They might live in a wild and unpredictable world, but with Meika, Raela, and Paka by his side, he felt safe and, in a way, invincible.

8

CAMARADERIE

As Koda grew, his life shifted from the carefree explorations of childhood to the responsibilities that came with maturity. Erek and Varo, Taron's sons, took a keen interest in teaching Koda the skills he would need to thrive in the forest. Koda admired both of them deeply: Erek's calm, steadfast presence and Varo's quick-witted adaptability gave Koda two contrasting role models, each with valuable lessons to impart.

One misty morning, Erek led Koda to a section of the forest thick with ferns and tall pines. He crouched, his keen eyes scanning the ground, before motioning for Koda to follow suit. "Look here," Erek said, pointing to a faint track in the soil. "What do you see?"

Koda examined the ground, studying the print. It was a delicate track, almost indistinguishable in the loose soil, but the faint marks of claw tips were visible. "Raccoon?" Koda guessed, his tone hesitant.

Erek nodded. "Good. And see how the soil is only slightly disturbed? It's a sign this track is fresh, made just before dawn." He gave Koda a small smile. "Remember, each track tells a story. The more you understand it, the more you'll know about what moves through this forest."

Koda took these words to heart, and for the rest of the morning, he followed Erek, observing and learning the subtle language of the forest floor. Every print, every bent blade of grass, held clues to the world around him. He felt a surge of pride at each small success and every correct guess, growing more confident in his ability to read the land.

Another day, Varo took Koda out to the river, where they watched fish darting beneath the surface. Varo pointed to a spot where the water was deeper, swirling in slow circles. "That's where you'll find the biggest fish," he explained. "They wait in the shadows, avoiding the stronger currents." He reached down, his hand poised above the water, waiting patiently before darting in to scoop up a shimmering fish with a practiced motion.

Koda's attempts were clumsier, but Varo's patient encouragement kept him trying. "It's about timing, Koda," he said with a grin. "Feel the water, sense where the fish is, and move when you feel that moment." After several tries, Koda managed to catch a fish, and Varo laughed in approval, clapping him on the shoulder.

One early summer morning, Erek and Varo invited Koda on a foraging trip that would take them near the river. Koda was excited by the opportunity, eager to show what he'd learned and to take on more responsibility. They moved through the forest with a quiet ease, communicating through hand signals and low vocalizations as they foraged for wild roots and edible greens. The air was fresh, filled with the earthy scents of moss and pine, and the murmur of the river grew louder as they approached the water's edge.

As they neared a bend in the river, Erek suddenly held up a hand, signaling for silence. Koda froze, his heart pounding as he followed Erek's gaze. On the opposite bank, partially obscured by the under-brush, stood a human—a fisherman, casting his line into the river with a steady, practiced motion. The man was tall and wore a camou-flage jacket, blending into the surroundings with unsettling effec-tiveness.

Koda felt his chest tighten. Though he had seen humans from a distance before, he had never been this close to one, and the sight filled him with an instinctive fear. He looked to Erek and Varo, who both stood still, their postures tense and alert.

"Stay close to the trees," Varo whispered. "We'll move slowly, staying out of his line of sight."

Koda nodded, his movements careful and deliberate as he stepped back, eyes never leaving the figure on the other side of the river. They skirted along the edge of the trees, moving with a stealth that only years of practice could provide. But just as they were about to reach the cover of denser foliage, a sharp snap echoed through the air—Koda had accidentally stepped on a dry twig.

The sound was faint, but it was enough. The fisherman looked up, his eyes narrowing as he scanned the opposite bank. Koda's heart raced, and he crouched low, pressing against a tree trunk. He held his breath, every muscle tense as he waited, hoping the man hadn't seen him.

But the fisherman's gaze lingered, his expression puzzled as he took a few cautious steps closer to the riverbank. Koda's pulse thundered in his ears, and he could feel the adrenaline coursing through him. Erek signaled to him, pointing up, and Koda understood immediately. Without hesitation, he began to climb, his strong hands gripping the rough bark as he ascended into the branches, finding cover among the thick foliage.

From his vantage point, Koda watched the fisherman continue to search the opposite bank, his eyes scanning the trees where they had been standing moments before. Erek and Varo remained motionless below, blending into the shadows, their figures barely visible against the forest floor. After a few tense moments, the fisherman seemed to lose interest. He shrugged, muttering to himself as he turned back to his fishing rod.

Koda waited until the man's attention was fully on the river before he began his descent, moving carefully and silently until back on the ground. They continued moving, keeping a safe distance from the river until they were far from the fisherman's sight. Only then did they let themselves relax, sharing a glance of mutual relief.

"That was well done, Koda," Varo said quietly. "Quick thinking, and you moved fast."

Koda managed a small smile, though his heart was still racing. "I didn't want him to see us."

Erek placed a reassuring hand on Koda's shoulder. "You did the right thing. Out here, you have to trust your instincts. And today, they served you well."

That evening, back at the clan's home base, Koda couldn't contain himself. Words spilled from his mouth, tumbling over one another as he recounted their encounter to the elders. He gestured wildly, his hands mimicking the drama of the moment, his voice rising and falling with the excitement still buzzing in his veins. Kabota, Asha, Omaki, and Taron leaned in, giving him their full attention. Koda's eyes sparkled, his chest puffing slightly with pride as he described every detail, the brush of danger still fresh in his animated movements. "You handled yourself well, Koda," Kabota said, his tone filled with pride. "It's not every day that you come face-to-face with a human and manage to stay hidden."

Asha smiled, reaching out to ruffle Koda's hair. "You're growing up quickly, learning to be cautious and wise in these woods. We're proud of you."

Omaki, her gaze warm but thoughtful, added, "It's encounters like these that remind us to stay vigilant. Humans grow bolder every year, venturing deeper into our territory. We must be ready for anything."

Taron nodded. "The forest is changing, and so must we. But with each new generation, we gain strength. Koda, you are part of that strength now."

Koda beamed, his chest swelling with pride. The encounter with the fisherman had been a test of his courage, and though still young, he felt the first stirrings of what it meant to be a protector of his clan, just like his father and the elders before him. He knew he had much to learn, but with his family and his clan by his side, he was ready for whatever the forest might bring.

Koda's world was an ever-expanding canvas of colors, sounds, and sensations, and now, as he neared his first year, he found himself reflecting on all he had learned. It was a strange feeling, this understanding of time, of moments passing and experiences gathering within him like treasures. Just a year ago, he had been a small, fragile creature, clinging to his mother's hair, reliant on her strength and guidance. But now, he felt his own strength blooming, his mind sharpening as he learned to navigate the forest and the life he shared with the Hoh Clan.

The year had been one of discovery. Each member of the clan had taught him something unique, something vital, and these memories wove the fabric of his young life.

Omaki held a special place in Koda's heart. She was a quiet, observant figure, her wisdom rooted in the countless seasons she had witnessed. Koda had learned early on that Omaki's way of teaching was subtle, almost hidden. She rarely instructed directly; instead, she would tell stories, painting images of past events and the creatures of the forest. In those stories lay the lessons Koda would come to understand only with time.

One chilly morning, as the mist curled around the trees, Koda sat with Omaki on a moss-covered log. She was speaking of the seasons, her words a gentle reminder that everything in the forest had its time and place. Koda listened intently, mesmerized by her soft, rhythmic voice.

"Do you know why the leaves fall?" she asked, her gaze drifting to the towering maples whose leaves had turned to a vibrant red and gold.

Koda shook his head, eager to hear the answer.

"They fall to make way for new life," Omaki explained. "When they reach the forest floor, they become part of the soil, nourishing the roots of the trees they once adorned. And so, each season is not an end, but a beginning."

Koda nodded, understanding that Omaki's lesson was not only about leaves. She was teaching him about change, about accepting the cycles of life in the forest. He carried this knowledge with him in the months that followed, noticing the changes in the world around him with new eyes.

9

TEACHINGS

Koda crouched low, his hand brushing the earth as he traced the faint tracks of a deer. Erek's voice, steady and calm, echoed in his mind: *"Every animal leaves a trail. If you learn to see it, you'll understand its story."* The lesson wasn't just about tracking; it was about listening—to the land, to the subtle shifts in the forest's rhythm. Koda had learned to slow his breath, to quiet his thoughts, and let the forest speak.

His patience, though hard-won, had been honed under Omaki's watchful eye. She had taught him to sit still and let the wind carry its secrets, to notice the way the trees leaned or the underbrush whispered of movement. Once, while they sat in a silent grove, she had murmured, *"The forest reveals itself only to those willing to listen."* Koda never forgot the way her words seemed to weave into the very fabric of the trees around them.

Not all his lessons were quiet ones. Kabota's teachings came in sharp, decisive moments. He could still feel the rough bark under his claws the first time he marked the clan's territory, his father standing tall beside him. *"These marks tell others we're here,"* Kabota had said, his voice unyielding. *"They tell intruders this land is protected."* The pride that swelled in Koda's chest as he left his first mark burned brighter than the soreness in his arms.

But Kabota wasn't just a teacher of survival. On softer days, they wrestled in the clearing, Koda scrambling to match his father's strength and agility. Through laughter and mock defeat, Kabota taught him the art of balance, the precision of movement, and how to anticipate an opponent's next move. Those moments lingered, shaping Koda's confidence and connection to his father.

With Varo, every outing felt like stepping into a new story. One afternoon, Varo led him to a hidden waterfall deep within the forest, the sunlight breaking through the canopy to dance on the clear water. Koda's breath caught at the sight, but Varo grinned, always the teacher. *"The best things are often hidden,"* he said, crouching by the edge of the pool. *"You just have to be brave enough to find them."*

It wasn't all wonder, though. Varo had a way of turning excitement into lessons. The day they stumbled upon fresh bear tracks, Koda felt a prickle of fear as Varo's hand shot up, signaling silence. They froze, listening to the forest shift around them. *"Every creature has its space,"* Varo whispered, his body tense but calm. *"Respect it, and trust your instincts to guide you."* The retreat had been slow, deliberate, and left Koda with a deep understanding of how courage could coexist with caution.

Through it all, Koda grew—guided, shaped, and challenged by those around him. The playful daring of Varo, the quiet precision of Erek, the grounded strength of Kabota, and the patient wisdom of Omaki each carved something essential into him. The forest became more than home; it became a mirror of their lessons and the rhythms of his own growing instincts. Every step he took, every mark he left, every trail he followed deepened his connection to the land and the clan that had raised him to stand strong within it.

10

JOY

Koda hid behind a thicket, struggling to keep his laughter quiet as Paka darted past, oblivious to the ambush awaiting him. Meika's voice, calm but firm, carried through the trees. "Don't give away your position, Koda. He'll hear you." She stood nearby, scanning the surroundings, her steady presence grounding their play.

Moments later, Raela appeared silently at Koda's side, her keen eyes flicking toward the distant rustle that betrayed Paka's movements. "He's circling back," she murmured, barely above a whisper. Koda nodded, impressed yet again by how effortlessly she noticed things others missed.

Paka burst through the clearing, his face a mix of surprise and delight as Koda sprang out, tackling him to the ground. The two tumbled, laughter spilling into the crisp forest air. "I almost had you!" Paka shouted, wriggling free and darting off again, his boundless energy unstoppable.

Their games weren't just play—they were practice, woven into the fabric of their days. While racing through the forest or climbing towering trees, Meika kept them in check, her sense of responsibility guiding their adventures. She warned them of loose branches, reminded them to stay within the clan's boundaries, and always seemed to know when to steer them away from danger.

Raela, meanwhile, turned every moment into a lesson without even trying. As they tracked a deer through the underbrush one afternoon, she pointed out faint impressions in the soil that Koda hadn't noticed. "Look here," she whispered, motioning to a patch of disturbed leaves. "It veered left. See how the tracks are deeper on one side?" Koda followed her gaze, marveling at her ability to see what he couldn't.

Paka, of course, made every task an adventure. Whether he was daring them to scale the tallest tree or trying to balance on a fallen log over the stream, his wild enthusiasm was impossible to resist. "Koda, bet you can't make it to the top without looking down!" he shouted once, already halfway up a swaying cedar. Koda laughed and joined in, the thrill of the challenge outweighing his apprehension.

These moments weren't just diversions—they were the threads that held their bond together, shaping Koda in ways he barely realized. Through Meika, he learned to lead with care and caution. From Raela, he gained an appreciation for the subtleties of the world around him. And Paka's endless energy taught him to find joy even in the simplest moments.

As they regrouped by the river, Koda glanced around at his friends. Meika was perched on a rock, watching Paka try to skip stones, her expression equal parts amused and exasperated. Raela crouched by the water, tracing patterns in the mud with a stick, her thoughts clearly elsewhere. And Paka, ever the whirlwind, was already scheming their next adventure.

Koda felt a sense of gratitude. These weren't just friends—they were his family, his companions in a world that demanded strength and resilience. And even as the challenges of the forest loomed large, he knew that together, they could face whatever came next.

11

PRESENCE

As Koda entered his second year, the mysteries of the forest continued to unfold around him, and with them, the curious —and sometimes unsettling—presence of humans. He had grown accustomed to hearing about them from the older sasquatches, who spoke of the humans' tools, strange habits, and the odd, clumsy ways they moved through the forest. Encounters with humans were rare but always treated with caution and respect within the clan. Omaki and Taron taught that the humans were not to be feared outright, but they were unpredictable, and their presence warranted vigilance.

But to Koda and the rest of the younger members of the clan, these tales of humans stirred curiosity and trepidation. They wondered about these strange beings who left unnatural trails through the woods, who sometimes made loud sounds and lights that disturbed the night. And as much as they were taught to avoid humans, Koda and the other juveniles couldn't resist a little fun at the humans' expense.

One late summer afternoon, Meika led Koda, Raela, and Paka to a narrow trail where humans occasionally passed. She explained that her father, Taron, had shown her the "art" of misleading humans to protect the clan, confusing them enough to keep them away from the clan's primary territory. Koda's eyes widened as Meika described a few of the tricks she'd learned.

"First lesson," Meika said with a grin, "leaving a single footprint." She lifted her large, hairy foot and placed it firmly into a patch of soft soil, pressing down to leave a clear, deep impression. She then carefully stepped back, using a nearby rock to avoid leaving a second footprint.

"Humans get so confused when they see only one print," Meika said, chuckling. "They think it's like some kind of ghost creature."

Paka and Raela giggled, eager to try it themselves. Koda watched closely, then carefully pressed his foot into the soil, pulling back to admire the single print he left behind. The mark was faint, but Meika nodded approvingly.

"They'll spend hours just trying to figure out where the other footprints went," Raela added, her eyes shining with mischief.

Next, Meika showed them how to make tree breaks—small but visible cracks or bends in saplings that humans would see as peculiar or unnatural. She gently twisted a young tree trunk until it splintered, creating an audible crack.

"These marks make humans think they're being watched," Meika whispered. "They don't know it's us, but it gives them a little scare, enough to make them cautious."

Koda felt a thrill run through him as he practiced making his own tree breaks along the path, imagining the humans' reactions. Though he hadn't had another encounter with them since the incident with the fisherman, he felt the weight of their presence. They were intruders, but strange ones, moving through the forest in ways that didn't make sense to him. Yet he was fascinated by the humans, especially the effect they had on his clan.

The four of them spent the rest of the afternoon playing their tricks along the trail, carefully weaving between the trees, leaving footprints and tree breaks in just the right places to make their marks clear but cryptic. By the time they made their way back to the clan's territory, Koda was exhilarated by the idea that the humans would be stumped by the signs they'd left behind.

The next time Koda found himself near humans, the situation was far less lighthearted. Late one autumn evening, he had gone with Meika, Raela, and Paka to explore a stretch of forest by the river. They had intended to meet up with Erek and Varo, who had gone ahead to scout the area. But as twilight descended, Erek and Varo were nowhere in sight, and the young sasquatches were left waiting near the water's edge.

Koda felt a faint unease as the shadows deepened, casting an eerie stillness over the forest. Just as he was about to suggest heading back, a strange, distant sound echoed through the trees. It was a long, drawn-out howl, followed by a series of knocks against the trees. The sound was foreign, chilling, and unlike any call Koda had heard from his clan.

Meika motioned for them to crouch down, her face tense. "Humans," she whispered. "They're trying to mimic our sounds."

Koda's heart hammered as he listened. The sounds were close enough that he could hear a faint murmur of human voices, broken up by more howls and tree knocks. Clearly, the humans were trying to lure them out. The younger sasquatches huddled together, unsure of whether to stay or run.

Suddenly, a beam of light cut through the trees, illuminating the underbrush with a strange, unnatural glow. Koda's eyes widened. He had never seen anything like it, as if the humans had brought daylight into the night.

"What is that?" Raela whispered, shrinking back.

"They're using tools," Meika said, her voice laced with worry. "I've heard my father talk about this. They have lights that let them see in the dark."

Koda felt a shiver of fear but also a strange fascination. These humans seemed to possess a kind of magic, a way of bending the forest to their will. The beam swept the ground, scanning the forest floor. Koda held his breath, hoping the darkness would conceal them.

But as the voices grew louder, he realized the humans weren't staying in one group—they were spreading out, moving around the young sasquatches in an attempt to flank them. They were being surrounded.

Meika gestured for them to move, signaling for silence as she led them away from the river and into a dense thicket of bushes. They moved as quietly as they could, their senses on high alert, but Koda could feel the human presence closing in on them. Another beam swept over their hiding spot, and for a heart-stopping moment, Koda thought they had been spotted.

"We need to keep moving," Meika mouthed, her eyes wide with urgency. She motioned for Koda and the others to follow her lead, crouching low and weaving through the underbrush. Koda's heart pounded as he crept forward, every sound amplified in his ears. The humans' howling and tree-knocking continued, echoing through the trees with an eerie persistence.

They made it a few more yards before they heard footsteps— heavy, crunching footsteps from all directions. The humans had split into small groups, methodically sweeping through the forest in search of them. Koda felt a rising panic as he realized just how close the humans were. He could smell them now, a strange, unfamiliar scent that set his nerves on edge.

"Up the trees," Meika whispered urgently, motioning for them to climb. "They never look up."

Koda and the others scrambled up the nearest tree, their claws digging into the bark as they ascended into the safety of the branches. From his perch, Koda watched as two humans passed right beneath him, their faces illuminated by the glow of their strange devices. One held a small object that emitted a red light, scanning it back and forth as if searching for some sign of their presence.

Koda held his breath, pressing himself against the trunk as the humans moved below. The red light flickered, passing over the ground before disappearing into the darkness.

After a few tense moments, the humans moved on, their foot-steps fading into the distance. Koda exhaled slowly, glancing over at Meika, who gave him a reassuring nod. But just as he thought they were safe, another beam of light appeared on the other side of the tree, illuminating Raela, who was hidden just a few branches away.

The light paused, as if the human had seen something unusual. Koda felt a surge of panic as he realized that Raela was partially exposed, her hair blending in with the shadows but still faintly visible. They had to act quickly or risk being discovered.

Meika motioned for them to climb higher, using the thick foliage to shield themselves from view. Koda followed her lead, silently ascending into the upper branches. Raela did the same, her small form blending into the shadows as she moved out of the light's reach.

The humans hesitated, their voices tense as they scanned the area, but after a few moments, they seemed to lose interest and moved on. Koda felt a wave of relief wash over him, but he knew they weren't safe yet. The humans were still close, and they would need to stay hidden until they could find a way to escape.

They waited in silence, listening as the humans' voices grew fainter. Finally, Meika signaled for them to climb down, her expression tense but determined. One by one, they descended, landing softly on the forest floor. Koda could feel the adrenaline coursing through him as they crept through the underbrush, moving as quickly and quietly as they could.

When they were far enough from the humans, Meika led them to a small, secluded clearing to catch their breath. Koda glanced around, relived they had evaded the humans without being seen.

"I can't believe they looked up," Raela whispered.

Paka nodded, his eyes wide with fear. "I've never seen humans like that before. They were... They were hunting us."

"We made it out because we stayed calm and used everything we've learned. Remember that, Koda. The forest is our home, but it can be dangerous too. You have to be ready for anything."

Koda nodded, feeling a newfound respect for Meika and the others. The experience had been frightening but taught him a valuable lesson: the forest was a place of both beauty and danger, and he would need to rely on his instincts, his courage, and the support of his clan to navigate it safely.

As they made their way back to the clan's territory, Koda felt a deep sense of pride in the skills he had learned and the strength he had gained from his family. The forest might be filled with threats, but he knew he was never alone—and with each encounter, he grew more prepared to face whatever challenges lay ahead.

12

RHYTHM

By the time Koda and the others returned to the clan's main territory, the sky had darkened, stars twinkling faintly through gaps in the trees. The young sasquatches were exhausted from the close call with the humans. They knew the clan elders would want to know every detail, and as they approached the main clearing, they saw Omaki, Taron, Kabota, and Asha waiting for them.

Omaki stepped forward. "You four were gone for longer than usual," she said gently. "Are you all okay?"

Koda nodded, though he could feel his limbs trembling. He took a deep breath, trying to find the words to describe what they had experienced. "Humans," he said finally, his voice hushed. "They were different this time. They had strange tools, lights that could see in the dark, and they... They were making our sounds. Howling, knocking on trees."

Taron exchanged a worried glance with Kabota. "They're getting bolder," he said. "And more dangerous."

Asha said to the group of youngsters. "You did well to get back safely, all of you. Tell us what happened, in your own words."

Taking turns, the young sasquatches recounted their ordeal in vivid detail, describing how the humans had split up, used lights to search the dark, and even managed to get close enough that Koda thought they had been spotted. Omaki listened intently, her gaze focused and thoughtful.

"These humans are learning," she said softly. "They've come to understand that we are here, that we leave signs, and now they're using what they know to try to find us. We must be even more careful now."

Koda shivered at the implications. He'd always seen humans as clumsy and unaware, but tonight had changed that view. These humans were hunting, actively searching for his clan, and it made him feel vulnerable in a way he hadn't before. A swell of pride rose within him. They had outmaneuvered the humans, relying on the skills he'd honed with the clan to remain unseen and find their way back to safety.

Omaki placed a hand on his head, ruffling his hair in a rare show of affection. "Koda, you're growing quickly, learning much. But always remember—curiosity has its limits. Stay vigilant and listen to your instincts. They'll guide you as much as the forest will."

Kabota and Asha shared a glance, nodding. Kabota knelt to look Koda in the eye. "Every encounter you have, every close call, teaches you more. One day, you'll be the one protecting this clan."

Koda felt his chest swell with pride at his father's words. He understood that tonight's experience was one of many lessons he'd carry with him. It wasn't just about surviving; it was about being strong, wise, and united with his family.

In the days that followed, the clan convened to discuss the increasing human presence and how they could avoid detection. Omaki and Taron emphasized the importance of leaving fewer signs and trails, creating an atmosphere of caution and teamwork that Koda hadn't experienced before. The elders and older clan members took time to teach the younger ones new ways to remain hidden, especially from humans using lights and strange tools.

Koda found himself particularly fascinated by Omaki's teachings on camouflage and silence. She explained that humans relied heavily on sight and sound, often overlooking details in their hurry. They'd practiced these skills as a family many times, but now they focused on specifics like blending with shadows and moving without disturbing the underbrush.

"Always move with the rhythm of the forest," Omaki instructed them one misty morning as she led the young sasquatches through a dense part of the woods. "If a branch creaks, let it pass before you move. If you hear a rustling, pause and listen. This is how we keep the forest's secrets safe from prying eyes."

Koda took these lessons to heart, applying them each time he ventured out with the other juveniles or his mentors, Varo and Erek. He felt himself becoming more attuned to the forest's sounds and movements, finding comfort in the way he could move without leaving a trace. It was as if he was merging with the forest itself, a silent watcher within its depths.

Despite their efforts, they still encountered the humans at times, particularly near the river. The humans seemed drawn to the water, their paths crisscrossing along the banks where the clan often foraged. During one of these excursions, Koda, along with Meika and Paka, were collecting mushrooms near the river when they heard the unmistakable murmur of human voices approaching.

Koda froze, glancing at Meika, who quickly signaled for them to move up the hill, away from the trail. They scrambled through the underbrush, staying low as the humans passed, their voices filled with laughter and curiosity. Koda forced himself to stay calm, remembering Omaki's advice.

When the humans finally moved on, Koda exhaled in relief, sharing a grin with Paka, who had been crouching beside him. "We did it," Paka whispered, his excitement barely contained. "I don't think they even noticed us."

Meika nodded. "See? The humans may be getting smarter, but we're still faster, quieter. We know this forest better than they ever could."

Koda felt renewed confidence, realizing their training was paying off. But he also understood that these encounters weren't just games. Every time they avoided detection, it was a small victory, a reminder that they were not only surviving but thriving in the face of this strange and unpredictable presence.

One evening, as dusk settled over the forest, the clan gathered around the main clearing, sharing stories and enjoying the calm night air. Koda was with Paka, recounting the time they'd seen a human fall into the river, splashing and struggling as they tried to regain their footing. They laughed, amused by the memory of the human's clumsy movements, when they were interrupted by a strange flash of light in the distance.

Everyone fell silent, turning their attention toward the source of the light. A series of bright flashes pierced the darkness, illuminating the trees in short, rhythmic bursts. Koda's hair prickled as he watched, his curiosity mixing with growing unease.

"What is that?" Raela whispered, moving closer to Meika, who looked just as perplexed.

Omaki stepped forward, her eyes narrowed as she observed the lights. "Humans," she said quietly. "It's some sort of signal, but it's different from their usual lights."

Koda felt a surge of curiosity. The humans' tools and behaviors were becoming more intricate, more confusing. He had seen their lights before, but this was new, something deliberate.

Taron motioned for the younger ones to stay back. "They're searching," he said to Kabota. "They're getting closer each night."

The adults decided to observe from a distance, positioning themselves at various vantage points to monitor the humans' movements. Koda was frustrated; he wanted to be part of this, to see these strange lights up close, but he knew better than to argue. So he stayed back with his friends, watching as the elders faded into the shadows, leaving them to wait.

13

HUMANS

A few nights later, Koda, Meika, Raela, and Paka found themselves in an unexpected encounter that would test every skill they had learned. They had ventured out to forage for late-season berries near the edge of the river, staying within the shadows of the trees, careful to move quietly.

But as they filled their hands with berries, a noise cut through the air—a distant shout, followed by the crack of a branch breaking. Koda's heart sank as he realized they had wandered too close to a group of humans. They were surrounded.

Without hesitation, Meika motioned them toward a thicket to hide. They crouched low, blending into the shadows, their hearts pounding as the humans drew closer. But this time, the humans were using the flashing lights, sweeping the beams across the forest floor in a deliberate search.

Koda tried to steady his breathing, remembering Omaki's advice. Stay still, listen to the forest. But as the lights approached, his instincts urged him to flee.

The humans moved slowly, their footsteps heavy and clumsy, but their lights made it impossible to escape undetected. They scanned the area, their voices hushed and tense, and Koda realized with a jolt of fear that they were getting closer—too close.

Meika gestured for them to separate, each of them moving to a different spot in the underbrush. Koda crawled toward a fallen log, pressing himself against the cool bark as the light passed over him. He held his breath, hoping the humans wouldn't spot him.

Just when he thought they might be safe, a second group of humans appeared on the other side of the clearing, trapping them. The young sasquatches exchanged panicked glances, realizing they were surrounded.

Koda's mind raced, searching for a way out. Then he remembered one of Varo's lessons: when all else fails, move up. Without a sound, he began to climb the nearest tree, motioning for the others to do the same. Meika, Raela, and Paka followed, their movements swift and silent as they ascended into the branches.

They waited in tense silence, perched high above the humans, watching as the beams of light swept beneath them. The humans muttered to each other, frustrated by their inability to find anything, unaware that their quarry was just overhead.

After what felt like an eternity, the humans finally retreated, their lights fading. The young sasquatches waited until their footsteps had disappeared before descending from the trees, relieved.

Koda said, still shaken, "They're getting better at tracking us." Meika gave him a determined look. "As long as we stick together and remember what we've learned, we'll always be one step ahead."

Koda and the others shared their narrow escape with the clan, recounting the terrifying experience with fear and pride. Omaki listened carefully, nodding as they described evading detection using trees. She commended their quick thinking but reminded them of the growing human presence.

"We must be vigilant," she warned. "The forest is changing, and we must adapt."

Koda took her words to heart. The encounters with humans had taught him the importance of staying hidden, of blending with the forest, and of using every skill he had learned to protect himself and his clan. The humans would keep coming, but he was determined to face whatever challenges lay ahead.

With his family by his side and the strength of the clan guiding him, Koda felt ready. The forest was a place of beauty, danger, and mystery, and he was a part of it—forever bound to its secrets and its shadows.

PART II

14

HISTORY

The night was thick with fog, the mist coiling around the trees like ghostly tendrils. Koda sat by the mouth of the cave, listening to the faint sounds of his sleeping clan and the soft murmur of the forest outside. But then, as he listened, another sound pierced the night—a distant, mournful howl. He'd heard it before, echoing through the trees, stirring unease in his heart.

Adanowa.

Koda had never seen the rogue sasquatch up close, but the stories of his terror had already become legend within the clan. His presence lingered like a shadow on the edge of their territory, a reminder of the dangers that lurked beyond their familiar trails.

As the howl faded into silence, Koda glanced back into the cave, where his parents, Kabota and Asha, lay huddled close, sleeping under the watchful eye of the elders, Taron and Omaki. Koda turned to see Omaki watching him, her gaze thoughtful and steady.

"You heard it too, didn't you?" Koda whispered, his voice barely audible.

Omaki nodded. "Adanowa is restless tonight," she said softly. "He calls out, as he often does. But tonight... it feels different."

Kabota stirred, his eyes opening as he listened to Omaki. He sat up, turning to Taron, who nodded slowly. "It's time we told you," Taron said, looking between Kabota, Asha, and Koda, "the full story of Adanowa, of what drives him and why he wanders, forever seeking something he may never find."

Koda leaned forward. He had always known Adanowa was dangerous, that he had once been part of another clan, but never knew the details, the dark path that had led the rogue to their territory.

Taron took a deep breath, his gaze distant as he began to speak. "Adanowa wasn't always like this," he said, his voice filled with quiet sorrow. "There was a time when he was part of a clan back east, in the dense forests of Tennessee. His family roamed the Appalachian mountains, a place wild and beautiful, filled with ancient trees and hidden valleys."

Omaki nodded, her eyes softening with a trace of pity. "But Adanowa's life was marked by tragedy from the beginning," she added. "When he was young, barely older than you, Koda, his parents were hunted down by humans. They were a part of the first sasquatch clan in Tennessee to encounter humans on the Appalachian Trail."

Koda shivered as he imagined a young Adanowa, alone and grieving, left to survive in a world that had suddenly turned hostile.

Taron continued, his voice laced with a deep sorrow. "Humans had been curious about the trail for a long time, moving farther into the forests. But as they built camps and left trails through sasquatch territory, they grew suspicious of the beings they sensed but could not see. Adanowa's parents were careful—they avoided the trails, only watching from a distance. But one day, the humans noticed their tracks, strange and different from any other creature."

The clan listened intently as Taron described the tragic events that followed. The humans, fueled by curiosity and fear, had set up traps along the trail, hoping to catch a glimpse of the unknown beings that haunted their campsites. Although they were always vigilant, one night, they ventured too close. The humans spotted them, and a chase began—a relentless pursuit through the dense woods.

"They hunted them like animals," Omaki said softly, her voice trembling with anger. "His parents tried to escape, but the humans were many, armed with weapons and tools that lit up the night like daylight."

Koda's heart ached as he imagined the scene—the fear, the desperation, the final moments of Adanowa's parents as they tried to protect their child. "What happened to Adanowa?" he whispered, his voice barely audible.

Taron's gaze darkened. "He watched from the shadows, hidden in the hollow of a tree. He saw everything—the humans chasing his parents, the final struggle. And then... he was alone. An orphan, left to survive in a world that had taken everything from him."

Kabota and Asha exchanged a sorrowful glance, their hearts heavy with the knowledge of the pain that had shaped Adanowa's life. They could see how such a loss would leave a mark on a young sasquatch, how it would plant the seeds of anger and mistrust.

"Adanowa survived," Omaki continued, "but he was never the same. His heart grew hardened, filled with a simmering rage that only deepened as he grew older."

After the death of his parents, Adanowa wandered alone through the mountains, his anger festering into a dark resolve. He avoided the humans at first, but as he grew stronger, his fear turned into something else—a desire for revenge.

"He became a shadow on the Appalachian Trail," Taron explained, his voice low and haunted. "He would watch the hikers from a distance, studying their movements, waiting for the right moment to strike. He knew the trail better than any human, and he used that knowledge to his advantage."

Koda felt a chill as he listened, imagining Adanowa lurking in the shadows, his presence barely perceptible as he stalked the hikers who ventured too far from the safety of the trail. The rogue's first encounters were cautious, almost experimental. He would break branches, leave single footprints, create eerie sounds that left the hikers trembling with unease. But eventually, his rage grew stronger than his restraint.

"Adanowa began to hunt them," Taron said, his voice filled with a quiet horror. "He would wait until they were alone, vulnerable. And then he would strike."

The clan sat in stunned silence, each of them picturing the rogue's transformation from a grieving orphan to a vengeful predator. Koda felt fear for the monster Adanowa had become but pity for the creature he had once been.

Omaki continued, her gaze distant as she recounted the stories she had heard from other clans. "His actions drew the attention of nearby clans. They warned him, tried to reason with him, but Adanowa was consumed by anger. He would not listen. And so, one by one, the clans pushed him out, casting him into the wilderness, hoping he would disappear."

But Adanowa was determined. He left the Appalachians, wandering westward through forests and mountains, following a path that would eventually lead him to the Olympic Peninsula. Along the way, he had encountered other sasquatch clans; some tried to help him, others drove him away, fearing his violent tendencies.

As Adanowa journeyed across the country, conflict and struggle marked his path. He had lost his family, home, and sense of belonging, and in their place, he carried only anger and mistrust of both humans and his own kind.

Taron spoke of these encounters, his voice filled with a quiet reverence for the power and resilience of the rogue sasquatch. "He didn't care for alliances or friendships—he was driven by something darker, something that could not be reasoned with."

Koda listened, mesmerized by the story of Adanowa's journey. He could feel the weight of the rogue's anger, the isolation that had shaped him into a creature of fear and violence.

In the dense forests of Kentucky, Adanowa had encountered a clan that guarded their territory fiercely. They were wary of outsiders and recognized the danger that Adanowa posed. When he refused to leave, a brutal confrontation ensued, with Adanowa barely escaping alive. He had learned then that not all sasquatch were willing to accept him, that his rage made him an outcast among his own kind.

But despite his physical and emotional wounds, Adanowa pressed on. He passed through the Great Plains, crossing rivers and mountains, always westward, his path a twisted journey of survival and vengeance. He encountered humans along the way, and each encounter fueled his hatred, reminding him of the night his parents had been taken from him.

It was in the Rocky Mountains that Adanowa's descent into darkness became complete. The vast wilderness offered him solitude but also brought him face-to-face with other sasquatch clans, each wary of the lone stranger who had wandered into their territory.

One such encounter had nearly cost Adanowa his life. He had stumbled into a clan's hunting grounds, his scent alerting the alpha to his presence. The alpha, a massive sasquatch named Garok, confronted Adanowa, challenging him for his recklessness. But Adanowa's anger had taken over. He fought back with a ferocity that shocked even Garok, refusing to back down even when outmatched.

The fight was brutal, leaving Adanowa scarred and battered, but it also solidified his status as a rogue, a creature of violence and rage who would not bow to any authority. He left the Rockies, his body marked with the scars of his battles, his heart hardened to the world around him.

By the time he reached the Olympic Peninsula, Adanowa had become a legend among the sasquatch clans. His name was spoken in whispers, a warning to those who would cross his path. He was a creature of the shadows, a being of darkness who roamed the forests with a single purpose—to survive, and to make the humans pay for the pain they had inflicted on him.

When Adanowa finally arrived in the Olympic Peninsula, he found a land as wild and untamed as his own heart. The dense forests, the towering mountains, and the vast stretches of wilderness offered him the solitude he craved. But even here, he could not escape the presence of humans. They ventured into his territory, leaving trails and campsites, their presence a constant reminder of the life he had lost.

"He settled here, but his rage never faded," Omaki explained. "He has been hunting humans ever since, striking fear into the hearts of those who venture too close. And now... he is here, haunting these woods, a reminder of the pain that lives within him."

Koda shivered as he listened to the final part of Adanowa's story. He understood now why the rogue was so feared, why his presence cast a shadow over the clan. Adanowa was more than a threat—he was a creature shaped by tragedy, a being whose heart had been consumed by anger and loss.

"This is why we must be vigilant," Kabota said softly. "Adanowa may be dangerous, but he is also lost, a creature who has been hurt in ways we cannot imagine. We must respect him, but we must also protect ourselves."

Asha nodded, her expression filled with determination. "We will keep our family safe, no matter what."

As the clan sat lost in thought, Koda felt a deep sense of understanding. Adanowa was not just a monster—he was a tragic figure, a reminder of the dangers that lurked in the world beyond their forest.

But he also felt a renewed purpose. He would take everything he had learned, every skill he had honed, and use it to protect his clan, to ensure that they would never face the same fate as Adanowa.

And as the howls of the rogue echoed through the night, Koda knew that he was ready. Ready to protect his family from the darkness that had claimed Adanowa's soul.

15

GATHERING

The summer of Koda's third year arrived with a vibrancy that filled the forest with life. The trees were lush and green, their branches heavy with new growth, and the air hummed with the sounds of creatures busy with their own lives. For Koda and his family, this season marked a special time—the gathering of nearby sasquatch clans, a tradition that allowed the clans to trade, share knowledge, and strengthen the bonds between their families. It was a time of celebration and preparation, an opportunity to work together to ensure everyone's survival through the winter.

Koda had heard stories of these gatherings from Omaki and Taron, who spoke of the distant clans that would travel through the dense forests to meet at the heart of the Olympic Peninsula. He had never been part of one himself, but he could feel the excitement and anticipation in the air. Kabota and Asha prepared him, teaching him about the customs and etiquette of these meetings. The gathering would be a chance to learn from others, to share their strengths, and to contribute to the welfare of the entire sasquatch community.

As dawn broke over the forest, the clan set out, following familiar trails that led to a vast clearing surrounded by towering trees and sheltered from the wind. Koda's heart raced as they approached, his mind buzzing with curiosity and excitement. He had grown stronger over the past year, his skills honed by the challenges he had faced, and he felt ready to meet the other clans, to learn from them, and to find his place in the larger world of his people.

As they entered the clearing, Koda's eyes widened. Several clans had already arrived, scattered around the clearing in small groups, each engaged in quiet conversations or preparing for the days ahead. Koda saw subtle differences in the other sasquatches—their hair colors, their builds, and the distinct markings that told the story of their lives in the forest.

Kabota and Asha led Koda to one of the groups, where a tall, silver-haired sasquatch with wise, piercing eyes was speaking to Omaki. The elder looked up as they approached, his expression softening with warmth.

"Kabota, Asha," he greeted them, nodding respectfully. "It has been too long."

Kabota smiled, clasping the elder's shoulder. "It has, old friend. This is my son, Koda."

The elder's gaze shifted to Koda, his eyes filled with curiosity and approval. "Koda, I am Jarok. I lead the Stone Ridge Clan, and it is an honor to meet you."

The Stone Ridge Clan was known for their endurance and survival skills. In preparation for the hunt, Jarok led his family in reinforcing the traditions and strategies that had kept them alive through harsh winters and lean years. Their knowledge of difficult terrain and ability to navigate the rockier parts of the northern woods would be crucial in the coming hunt.

Koda lowered his head in respect, he raised his gaze with pride to meet Jarok's. The elder stood tall, his silver-streaked hair catching the light, each scar on his rugged frame a testament to battles fought and hardships endured. Stories of the Stone Ridge Clan had reached Koda before—tales of their resilience, their ability to thrive in the unforgiving rocky terrain north of the peninsula, where winters bit hard and resources were sparse.

Jarok's reputation was legendary. As a young sasquatch, he had ventured far beyond his territory, gathering survival knowledge from the farthest reaches of the forest. That experience shaped him into a leader who could navigate the challenges of the northern mountains with a steady hand and an unyielding spirit. He wasn't just the head of his clan; he was their shield, their compass, the force that held them together through the harshest storms.

Koda could feel the weight of Jarok's presence—the quiet authority in his posture, the wisdom in his piercing gaze. It wasn't just respect the elder commanded; it was trust, earned through years of sacrifice and leadership. Standing before him, Koda couldn't help but feel inspired, as though Jarok's strength was something he, too, could aspire to.

Beside Jarok stood two younger sasquatches, his sons, who regarded Koda with interest. The elder of the two, a broad-shoul-dered sasquatch named Rokan, had hair the color of burnt sienna, his gaze steady and calm. He was known for his strength and endurance, a hunter who could travel for miles without tiring. His broad shoulders and powerful frame allowed him to take down large prey, often single-handedly when necessary. Rokan was quiet and introspective, often lost in thought, but his loyalty to his family was unwavering. His tracking abilities and patience made him an invalu-able asset during hunts, especially in the treacherous northern woods.

His brother, Sika, was leaner, his hair a darker shade, almost black, with eyes that sparkled with intelligence and curiosity. Sika was a skilled tracker, known for his sharp senses and his ability to navigate even the trickiest terrain. Sika's curious and adventurous spirit led him to explore beyond their territory, where he learned to navigate new terrain and identify subtle signs of animal presence. His skills would be essential in scouting the area for elk trails, finding water sources, and ensuring the clan's safety.

Jarok introduced them, his voice filled with pride. "These are my sons, Rokan and Sika. They will be joining the hunt, as will I. It has been some time since we hunted together."

Koda greeted them, feeling a connection with Sika, whose

curiosity and agility reminded him of his own. Rokan, though more reserved, gave Koda a respectful nod, and Koda sensed the strength and reliability in his presence.

Jarok's mate, Maera, was the clan's healer, her knowledge of herbs and natural remedies unmatched. Her gentle demeanor and nurturing nature made her beloved within her clan, and even among the other clans, her skills were highly respected. She carried a pouch of dried herbs and roots with her, always prepared to treat wounds or illnesses. Maera would offer her skills to anyone in need during the gathering, sharing her knowledge with the younger sasquatches interested in herbal medicine.

Lura and Terak, Rokan and Sika's younger siblings, were only a few years apart, both full of curiosity and eager to learn from their elders. Though still too young to go on the hunt, they helped in small ways, collecting supplies and observing the clan's activities. Lura idolized Sika, often trying to mimic his tracking skills, while Terak had a deep admiration for Rokan and wanted to be a great hunter himself someday.

16

WARMTH

As they spoke, another group approached—a family with a striking appearance, their hair a rich, russet hue that gleamed in the sunlight. At their head was Marla, the matriarch of the Red Valley Clan, known for her warmth and wisdom. She was accompanied by her mate, Torik, a sturdy and gentle sasquatch with a calm demeanor. Their daughter, Nira, was young, around Koda's age, her bright eyes filled with adventure and wonder.

Marla greeted Omaki and Taron with a warm smile. "It is a blessing to be together again," she said, her voice soft and soothing. "We have much to share."

Koda exchanged a shy greeting with Nira, who smiled back, her curiosity mirroring his own. She had grown up in the lush valley south of the peninsula, a place where the forest was dense and the rivers ran clear and cold. Her clan was known for their knowledge of plants and herbs, and Marla was a skilled healer in her own right who often traded her remedies with other clans for food and resources.

As more clans arrived, the clearing buzzed with energy and anticipation. Koda took in each new face, learning their names, stories, and unique skills. There was Tyrek, the fierce but kind-hearted leader of the Riverbend Clan, whose people were expert fishers and had an uncanny ability to find hidden water sources even in the driest of seasons. And there was Lora, a quiet and contemplative sasquatch from the Mistwood Clan, whose family lived in the misty, shadowed forests on the eastern edge of the peninsula. Her knowledge of the forest's hidden paths was unmatched, and her people were known for their ability to move undetected through even the densest underbrush.

Koda felt a sense of awe and belonging as he listened to the stories of each clan, understanding for the first time the vast network of families that shared his world. These clans were his people, connected by a shared history and a mutual respect for the land that sustained them. He could feel the pride and strength that bound them together, a bond that would guide them through whatever challenges lay ahead.

The Olympic Peninsula held a quiet but vibrant network of sasquatch clans, each family connected by ancient traditions and shared ancestry. When they gathered each summer, it was more than a mere meeting—it was a renewal of bonds, a celebration of their existence in a world that often threatened their survival. This gathering brought together four clans, each with its own customs, strengths, and colorful personalities.

As the clans settled into the clearing, Koda made note of each individual as they arrived. It was rare to see so many of his kind at once, and the experience filled him with awe and excitement.

The Red Valley Clan, led by Marla, brought warmth and healing to the gathering. Living in a fertile valley south of the peninsula, their territory was rich with plant life, and they had developed a deep understanding of the forest's natural resources. The Red Valley Clan specialized in foraging, gathering plants and herbs for both food and medicine, and their knowledge was invaluable to the other clans. As the matriarch, Marla held the role of healer and spiritual leader within her clan. She had taught each of her family members about the forest's plants and their uses, instilling a respect for nature that guided their every action. Known for her remedies, she often shared her knowledge with other clans, and her presence was a calming force during the gatherings.

Marla's mate, Torik, was responsible for scouting and foraging within their territory. His ability to find food in even the most barren stretches of land had sustained their clan through difficult seasons. Torik's sturdy build and keen sense of smell allowed him to locate edible plants and water sources from a distance. During the hunt, he would work with Sika to locate the best trails and ensure the clan's safety.

Nira, Marla's daughter and Koda's age, was an apprentice healer under her mother's guidance. Though still learning, she showed a natural talent for identifying and using medicinal plants. Her curiosity and eagerness to learn endeared her to the older members, and she spent much of her time collecting plants and assisting Marla with healing preparations. Nira was adventurous, always eager to join the others in their exploration, and she formed a quick friendship with Koda, sharing her knowledge of plants and herbs.

Kerr and Miko, younger relatives of Marla and Torik, were skilled foragers and essential members of the clan's daily life. Kerr was analytical and meticulous, often memorizing the locations of specific plants and mapping the valley in his mind. Miko, his sister, was more impulsive but had an intuitive sense of direction and an uncanny ability to locate food sources. They would assist in preparing traps for the hunt and ensuring that the gathered herbs and roots were shared with the other clans as needed.

The Red Valley Clan's deep understanding of plants and natural resources made them invaluable during the gathering. Marla and her family shared their knowledge freely, ensuring that every clan could benefit from the valley's bounty. Their expertise would prove essential in providing sustenance and medicine for all.

17

VITALITY

The Riverbend Clan was a lively and robust group, their territory lying along the banks of a wide river that wound through the western edge of the peninsula. Known for their fishing skills and resourcefulness, they brought an element of vitality to the gathering, their laughter and energy infectious. Led by Tyrek, they were a close-knit family, each member contributing to the clan's well-being.

Tyrek was a broad-shouldered sasquatch with a hearty laugh and a jovial nature, though he was serious about his responsibilities as clan leader. His people's survival depended on the river, and he had taught his family to fish and gather water plants for food. Tyrek's strength and patience were legendary, and he often took charge during the gatherings, helping to organize activities and keep spirits high.

Tyrek's mate, Kala, was known for her skill in preparing the fish and plants that sustained their clan. Her expertise extended beyond foraging, as she had developed ways of drying and preserving food for the winter months. Kala's knowledge of preserving techniques made her an essential part of the gathering, as she would teach others how to store their bounty to last through the colder seasons.

Liam, Tyrek's nephew, was an enthusiastic fisherman. Though young, he was skilled with the nets and tools they used to catch fish along the river. Liam had a boisterous personality, and he enjoyed sparring with Koda and the other younger sasquatches, always eager to prove his strength. During the gathering, he worked closely with Tyrek and Kala, helping to gather supplies and assisting in any way he could.

Ellar, Tyrek's younger brother, was quiet and observant, known for his ability to read the currents of the river and predict the movements of fish and game. His knowledge of the river made him an excellent scout, and he was responsible for ensuring the clan's safety while they fished. Ellar's calm presence and skill in reading signs of weather changes and animal activity made him a trusted member of the group, and he shared his insights freely with the other clans.

The Riverbend Clan brought a spirit of joy and resilience to the gathering, their expertise in fishing and preservation a valuable asset. They shared their techniques with the other clans, ensuring that everyone could make the most of the river's resources.

18

MISTWOOD

The Mistwood Clan, hailing from the dense, shadowy forests of the eastern peninsula, had long been a ghostly presence in the world, their movements as elusive as the mist that clung to their homeland. Masters of stealth and survival, their role in the gathering of the clans was both crucial and understated, a blend of silent guardianship and calculated precision.

As the clans prepared for the hunt, the Mistwood scouts melted into the forest, their presence detectable only by the faint rustle of leaves or the fleeting glimpse of movement that vanished before it could be confirmed. It was said the Mistwood Clan could navigate blindfolded through the fog, their feet unerringly finding paths invisible to others. They carried an unspoken promise of protection, ensuring that no unwelcome eyes would fall upon the gathered clans.

Lora, the clan's matriarch, had orchestrated their movements with a precision born of years of mastery. Her plans were executed seamlessly, the Mistwood members weaving in and out of the shadows to map the safest paths and eliminate risks. She communicated not through grand speeches but with gestures and glances that conveyed volumes. Under her guidance, the forest itself seemed to conspire to hide the clans, swallowing their tracks and muffling their sounds.

As the hunt commenced, the Mistwood Clan's contributions became clear. They were the unseen edge of a blade, sweeping ahead of the hunters to clear the way. Lora's strategies kept the clans one step ahead of wandering humans and potential threats. Her mate, Bara, supplied the knowledge of edible plants and medicinal herbs that sustained the scouts, while whispers of his herbal remedies circulated among the gathered clans.

The younger generation of the Mistwood Clan, led by Lora's children, embraced their roles with unwavering focus. Talin's keen senses and unerring aim made him a silent predator, his traps providing vital resources for the hunt. Meanwhile, Sari's ghostlike movements ensured that no territory was left unchecked. The boundaries of the hunting grounds were secure under her vigilant watch, her silent reports relayed through cryptic signals that only the Mistwood Clan could decipher.

While others might not see their work directly, the results were irrefutable. The Mistwood Clan had created a perimeter of safety and secrecy, allowing the clans to move freely and focus on the hunt. Their mastery of the shadows was not just a skill—it was a vital force that kept the clans protected, unseen, and ready for anything. .

19

THE GREAT HUNT

As the sun set, the clan leaders discussed the great hunt. This was a tradition that allowed the clans to work together to bring down large game, ensuring plentiful food for winter. The leaders spoke in low voices, strategizing and assigning roles, their gazes serious and focused.

Jarok spoke first, his voice steady and commanding. "The elk have been plentiful this year, moving closer to the river where we have easier access. We will need a coordinated effort to take down enough to feed all of our clans."

Taron nodded, his gaze sweeping over the gathered sasquatch. "Each clan will contribute its strengths. The Stone Ridge Clan will drive the elk toward the river, using their endurance and strength to keep the herd moving in the right direction."

Marla stepped forward, her expression calm and confident. "The Red Valley Clan will be ready with traps along the river's edge. We've scouted the area and marked the best spots for an ambush."

Omaki nodded, glancing at the young sasquatches joining the hunt. "Our younger ones will watch and learn, assisting where needed and staying close to their families."

Koda felt a thrill as he listened to the plan, eager to be part of such an important event. This would be his first hunt with the other clans, a chance to prove his skills and contribute to the welfare of his people. He glanced at Sika and Nira, who were equally excited, their eyes bright with anticipation.

With the roles assigned, the clans dispersed to prepare for the hunt. Koda joined his family as they reviewed their roles, gathering tools and weapons they had crafted from stone and wood. Kabota showed him how to sharpen the edges of a stone blade, explaining the importance of having a strong weapon when hunting large game.

"This hunt will be unlike anything you've done before," Kabota said with pride and caution. "Remember to stay with the group and follow the plan. There is strength in unity."

Koda nodded, absorbing his father's words. He felt a sense of responsibility settle over him, knowing that this hunt was not just for his family but for the entire community. It was a test of his skills, his courage, and his loyalty to the clan.

The next morning, the clans gathered at the edge of the clearing, their forms blending with the shadows as they prepared for the hunt. The air was thick with anticipation, a sense of purpose that filled each of them with determination. They moved in silence, their footsteps light and careful as they followed the trails that would lead them to the hunting grounds near the river.

As they neared the area where the elk were known to graze, the clans split into their assigned roles. Jarok and his sons took the lead, positioning themselves on one side of the clearing where they would begin to drive the elk toward the river. The Red Valley Clan spread out along the edges of the river, setting up traps and creating barriers that would funnel the elk into a narrow path.

Koda stayed close to Kabota as he scanned the area. He could feel the presence of the other clans around him, each of them moving with precision and purpose. It was a carefully coordinated effort, a dance of strength and strategy that relied on the skills and instincts of every member.

Jarok signaled to the others, and the hunt began. The Stone Ridge Clan moved forward, their large forms creating a wall that channeled the elk toward the river. The elk were massive creatures, their antlers stretching wide as they snorted and stomped, sensing the presence of the hunters. But the Stone Ridge Clan was relentless, their movements steady and controlled, forcing the herd to move in the direction they wanted.

Koda watched in awe as the Red Valley Clan sprang into action, their traps springing up as the elk approached the river. The large animals hesitated, their instincts telling them to flee, but the traps and barriers prevented them from escaping. The clans closed in, surrounding their prey with a precision that left no room for error.

As the first elk broke free, Koda saw his moment. With a nod from Kabota, he moved forward, his body tense and focused. He felt the weight of his stone blade in his hand, its edge sharp and ready. The elk charged, its powerful legs propelling it forward, but Koda held his ground, waiting for the right moment.

With a swift, practiced motion, he struck, his blade finding its mark. The elk stumbled, its massive form swaying as it fell to the ground. Koda felt a surge of pride as he looked at his father, who nodded in approval.

The hunt continued, the clans working together to bring down several elk, their teamwork and skill evident in every movement. By the time the hunt ended, the clearing was filled with the bounty of their efforts—a supply of meat and hides that would hopefully sustain them through the winter.

As the clans gathered around their catch, the leaders met to discuss how the bounty would be divided. It was a solemn moment, one that required fairness and respect for the contributions of each clan. Jarok, Taron, and Marla led the discussion, each of them acknowledging the efforts of the others and ensuring that every clan received an equal share.

Koda watched the leaders carefully divide the meat, hides, and bones, each piece going to a family who would use it to survive the winter. It was a moment of unity, a reminder of the strength that came from working together.

As the last pieces were distributed, the clans gathered around the fire, sharing stories and celebrating their success. Koda felt a deep sense of belonging as he listened to the laughter and voices of his people, each bound by family, friendship, and survival.

20

PARTING

As summer gave way to fall, the clans prepared to part ways, each returning to their own territory to prepare for winter. It saddened Koda to say goodbye to his new friends, promising to see them again at the next gathering.

But as he returned to his clan's territory, his heart filled with pride and gratitude. He was part of something greater, a community that would stand by him, protect him, and teach him the ways of the forest. And as the first snow fell, Koda looked forward to the future, knowing he was ready for whatever challenges lay ahead.

Snow blanketed the Olympic Peninsula in a thick, quiet shroud, muting the forest and signaling the start of the harshest season. The world had transformed overnight into a landscape of white, the trees weighed with snow, their branches creaking under the weight. For Koda and his clan, this winter would test their endurance, not only against the bitter cold but also against their growing unease.

Adanowa's presence had been a distant threat for as long as Koda could remember. But with each winter, as food became scarcer and the nights longer, the fear of the rogue's return intensified. The stories told cast Adanowa as a ghostly figure who prowled the edge of their territory, a lone shadow watching and waiting, a creature driven by rage and loss. And now, as Koda huddled close to his family in the warmth of their den, he could feel the weight of that threat pressing down on him.

Omaki, ever watchful, had already gathered the clan to discuss the measures they would take to stay safe during the winter months. Every night, they would post lookouts, each member taking turns to stand guard, listening for any signs of movement in the forest beyond. They would ration their food carefully, venturing out only when necessary, and avoid leaving tracks that could lead a predator back to their cave.

Despite these precautions, Koda saw the worry on the faces of his family. Kabota and Asha exchanged glances filled with silent concern, and Taron, though composed, often stared into the distance, as if waiting for some unseen enemy to appear.

The clan's unity and strength had taken on a tense edge, their movements cautious, their conversations laced with fear. For Koda, it was a reminder that the dangers they faced went beyond the cold and hunger—there was a darkness lurking in the forest, and it had a name.

Adanowa.

21

WINTER

To pass the long winter nights, the clan often gathered in their cave, sharing stories that kept their spirits alive and reminded them of their heritage. But this winter, the stories often turned to Adanowa, each tale darker and more chilling than the last.

Koda listened intently as Omaki spoke of Adanowa's strength and cunning, of his skill in tracking and evading, and of the countless encounters he had survived over the years. She described him as a creature shaped by the harshest of experiences, a being whose rage had transformed him into something other than a sasquatch—something dangerous and relentless.

"It is said that he can move without leaving a trace," Omaki said, her voice barely above a whisper. "He watches from the shadows, waiting for his moment to strike. And he fears nothing—not even death."

Koda felt a chill as he listened, the weight of Adanowa's presence settling heavily in his mind. He could sense the tension in the air, the unspoken fear that Adanowa might one day decide to target their clan. The rogue's actions were unpredictable, his motives inscrutable, and the knowledge that he roamed the same forest as them was enough to keep them on constant alert.

The elders reminded the younger ones of the importance of caution, urging them to stay close to the den and avoid drawing attention. But even with these warnings, Koda couldn't shake the feeling that Adanowa was out there, watching, waiting for the right moment.

As the days grew colder, the clan's food stores from that summers hunt began to dwindle, forcing them to venture out into the snow-covered forest to hunt and forage. These trips were carefully planned, each member assigned a role to ensure their safety and efficiency. Kabota and Asha, as the strongest hunters, would lead the group, while Taron and Omaki scouted ahead, searching for signs of danger.

Koda was assigned to help with tracking. He moved quietly, his senses heightened as he scanned the snow for tracks, his breath visible in the cold air. The silence of the forest was oppressive, each sound amplified by the stillness, and he had the distinct feeling that he was being watched.

They found a trail of deer tracks leading deeper into the woods, and Kabota signaled for the group to follow. But as they moved forward, Koda noticed something strange—an impression in the snow that looked like a footprint, larger than any animal he knew.

His heart pounded as he crouched to examine it, realizing it was not a deer track but a sasquatch print. He looked up at Kabota, who nodded grimly.

"Adanowa," Kabota whispered. "He's been here recently."

The group tensed, their senses on high alert as they continued their search. They moved with caution, scanning, but the forest kept silent, holding its breath. The threat of Adanowa lingered over them like a shadow, forcing them to move quickly, to gather what they needed and return to the safety of their den.

Each trip out of the den became a test of nerves, the fear of Adanowa adding tension to their already precarious existence. Koda felt his instincts sharpening, his senses attuned to the slightest sound, the faintest scent. He knew that one mistake could mean disaster, that Adanowa was out there, watching and waiting for any sign of weakness.

22

THE WATCHERS

One evening, as the sun dipped below the horizon and twilight bathed the forest, Kabota approached Koda with a serious expression.

"It's time, Koda," he said. "Tonight, you will take your first turn at keeping watch."

Koda nodded, understanding the responsibility that came with the role. He followed his father to the edge of the den, where they positioned themselves on a small ledge overlooking the forest. The night was still, the stars bright against the dark sky, and Koda could feel the cold seeping into his bones.

Kabota showed him how to stay alert, how to listen to the subtle sounds of the forest and watch for any signs of movement. They sat in silence, their breaths visible in the frigid air, their eyes scanning the darkness.

As the hours passed, Koda drifted into a trance, focused on the forest around him. Every rustle of leaves, every creak of a branch shot adrenaline through him, but he reminded himself to stay calm, to trust in the skills he had learned.

Just before dawn, as the first light filtered through the trees, Koda heard a faint sound—a distant familiar howl. It was Adanowa's call, a low, mournful wail that echoed through the forest, a reminder of his presence and the threat he posed.

Koda held his breath, listening as the howl faded into silence. He glanced at Kabota, who nodded solemnly, his expression a mixture of sadness and resolve.

"That's his way of reminding us," Kabota said. "He wants us to know he's still out there, watching."

Koda felt a surge of determination as he listened to his father's words. He understood now that this winter would be a test of his courage and his commitment to his family. He would need to stay vigilant, to protect his clan from the darkness that lurked in the forest.

23

TACTICS

As the days passed, the clan worked together to develop strategies for staying safe and avoiding Adanowa's attention. Omaki and Taron, with their wealth of experience, led the discussions, their voices calm and reassuring as they outlined the steps each member would take in the event of an encounter with the rogue.

They agreed to limit their trips outside the den, focusing on conserving their energy and rationing their food stores. Each member was assigned a specific role—some would guard the entrance, others would gather supplies, and the younger ones were taught to hide in specific spots within the cave where they would be safe.

Koda listened intently, memorizing every detail, every instruction. He understood the danger that Adanowa posed, and he was determined to do his part to protect his family.

One afternoon as the clan gathered, Taron spoke of Adanowa's tactics, his methods of stalking and ambushing his prey. He explained how Adanowa used the forest to his advantage, moving through the shadows, leaving no trace.

"He is cunning," Taron warned, his gaze sweeping over the younger members. "He knows these woods as well as we do, and he has no mercy for those who cross his path. We must be prepared for anything."

The clan listened in silence, each feeling the weight of Taron's words. Koda felt a renewed sense of purpose, a determination to stay strong and vigilant. He knew winter would be long and difficult but was ready to face the challenges ahead.

One icy morning, as Koda and Kabota ventured out to scout, they noticed a strange silence in the forest. The usual sounds of birds and small animals were absent, and the air felt thick with tension. Kabota motioned for Koda to stay close, his expression wary as they moved through the snow-covered trees.

As they approached a clearing, Koda caught a faint scent on the wind—a musky, unfamiliar odor that made him stop suddenly. He glanced at his father, who nodded, his eyes narrowing.

"It's him," Kabota whispered. "Adanowa has been here."

They scanned the area, alert, but found no sign of the rogue. The forest remained silent, the snow undisturbed, and yet Koda felt the weight of Adanowa's presence, as if he were watching from the shadows.

They quickly gathered what they needed and returned to the den, their hearts heavy with the knowledge that Adanowa was closer than they had realized. The encounter reflected the harsh truth of the dangers they faced, a reminder that they could not afford to let their guard down.

As the winter wore on, the clan grew closer, their bond strengthened by the shared threat and the knowledge that they would need each other to survive. They spent long nights huddled together, sharing stories and laughter, their voices filling the cave with warmth.

Koda felt a deep sense of pride and gratitude for his family, for the strength and resilience that bound them together. He knew that they were more than a clan—they were a family, a community united by love and loyalty.

And as the snow continued to fall, blanketing the world in silence, Koda found comfort in the knowledge that they would face whatever challenges lay ahead together, their hearts filled with courage and their spirits unbroken.

The winter was harsh, and the danger was real. But Koda knew he was ready to face it, to protect his family from the darkness that lurked beyond the forest, and to ensure that they would survive, no matter what.

24

CONFRONTATION

The forest transformed as winter gave way to spring, the once-quiet woods now alive with the sounds of water rushing from melting snow, the calls of birds returning to nest, and the buds of new leaves unfolding in the canopy above. For Koda, this season always felt like a time of renewal, a chance for the forest and its inhabitants to heal and grow after the hardships of winter. But this year, something was different—there was a tension in the air, an ever-present unease that overshadowed the usual joy of spring.

Humans had begun to trickle back into the forest, their voices carrying through the trees as they followed the well-worn trails. In past years, the clan would be cautious, observing the humans from afar and avoiding their paths. But this year, they had a greater threat to worry about: Adanowa. Over the winter, Adanowa had prowled the edges of their territory, his howls echoing through the night, a chilling reminder of his presence and his growing hostility.

Omaki and Taron had warned the clan to stay vigilant, to avoid wandering too far from the den. But with the abundance of spring, the need to forage and hunt became urgent. The clan couldn't afford to stay hidden, not if they wanted to survive. And so, they made plans for a large hunt, gathering supplies and organizing scouting parties to locate prey and assess the surrounding territory.

One morning, Taron set out to scout the nearby valley, a lowland area where deer often gathered in spring. His task was to locate the herd and determine the safest route for the clan to take when the hunt began. Taron was experienced, his every step careful and measured, his senses attuned to the sounds and scents of the forest. He moved through the trees with practiced ease, his eyes scanning the ground for tracks, his ears alert for any signs of movement.

But as he reached the edge of the valley, a faint, familiar scent reached his nostrils.

Adanowa.

Taron froze, his muscles tensing as he scanned the trees, his eyes narrowing as he searched for any sign of the rogue sasquatch. He knew that Adanowa had grown bolder over the winter, his presence an ever-looming threat. But Taron had hoped the rogue would keep his distance, that the harshness of winter would have weakened him, forced him to retreat deeper into the wilderness. Yet here he was, lurking on the edge of their territory, his scent unmistakable.

A low growl echoed through the trees. Taron turned and spotted a massive, shadowy figure moving toward him. Adanowa stepped into the clearing, his form towering and imposing, his eyes gleaming with malice. His hair was matted and his body streaked with scars.

"Taron," Adanowa sneered, his voice a low, guttural rumble. "I've been watching you and your clan. So careful, so cautious. Yet here you are, alone."

Taron stood his ground, his gaze steady, his expression unreadable. "This territory is not yours, Adanowa. We have kept to our land, respected the boundaries. You have no reason to be here."

Adanowa let out a dark chuckle, his eyes glinting with malice. "Respect? Boundaries? Those mean nothing to me, old one. You should have learned that by now." He took a step forward, his massive form looming over Taron. "I am not bound by your clan's rules. I am free. And I take what I want."

Taron felt a surge of anger but kept his voice calm. "You are alone because you choose to be, Adanowa. But that does not give you the right to harm others."

Adanowa's expression darkened, his muscles tensing as he prepared to strike. "Others," he spat. "You think your clan is safe from me? You think your borders protect you? I am not some creature to be contained, Taron. I am a force of this forest, and I will take from it as I please."

Before Taron could respond, Adanowa lunged, his claws slashing through the air with deadly precision. Taron barely had time to react, raising his arms to deflect the blow, but the force of Adanowa's attack sent him stumbling backward.

The two titans clashed, their roars could be heard for miles as they grappled, each fighting for dominance. Adanowa's strength was brutal, his movements fast and relentless, each blow a bone-jarring impact. Taron fought back with everything he had, his years of experience guiding his movements, his instincts sharp as he evaded Adanowa's attacks.

But he knew he was outclassed.

Adanowa's rage was unmatched, his strength fueled by years of anger and bitterness. Taron could feel his own strength waning, his body growing weaker with each blow. He managed to land a powerful strike to Adanowa's ribs, but the rogue barely flinched, his eyes filled with a crazed determination that bordered on madness.

"You are weak, Taron," Adanowa growled. "Your clan has made you soft. You hide behind them, relying on their protection. But out here, you are nothing."

With a final, brutal strike, Adanowa's claws raked across Taron's chest, tearing through flesh and muscle, the pain blinding. Taron staggered back, his vision swimming as he felt himself falling, his body collapsing onto the forest floor.

As darkness closed in around him, he heard Adanowa's laughter, a cold, mocking sound that echoed in his mind, a haunting reminder of his failure.

25

DREAD

When Taron failed to return, the clan knew something was wrong. Omaki gathered the rest of the clan, filled with fear as she led them into the forest, following Taron's trail through the trees. It was Asha who spotted him first, her sharp eyes catching sight of a dark shape lying in the underbrush. She let out a cry, rushing forward as the others followed, their hearts sinking as they saw the extent of Taron's injuries.

Taron lay on the ground, his body battered and broken, his breathing shallow, his hair matted with blood. Omaki dropped to her knees beside him, her hands trembling as she touched his face, her voice choked with emotion.

"Taron," she whispered, her voice filled with sorrow. "What has he done to you?"

Taron's eyes flickered open, his gaze unfocused, his voice barely a whisper. "Adanowa... He is relentless. He... He will come for us."

Kabota knelt beside Taron, his expression grim as he examined the wounds, his heart sinking as he realized the severity of the injuries. "We need to get him back to the cave," he said, his voice steady but filled with a quiet urgency. "Asha, gather the herbs. We'll do everything we can."

They lifted Taron's weakened form, carrying him back to the cave with a sense of desperation, each of them filled with the fear that they were losing their leader, their friend. Koda stayed close to his father, his heart heavy with grief and anger, his mind racing as he struggled to process what had happened.

Back at the cave, Omaki, worked tirelessly to tend to Taron's injuries, using every herb and remedy at her disposal to ease his pain and stop the bleeding. She applied poultices to his wounds, her hands gentle yet firm as she worked, her expression focused and determined.

Omaki stayed by Taron's side, her heart breaking as she watched him struggle for each breath, his once-strong body now weakened and frail. She held his hand, whispering words of comfort, her voice filled with love and sorrow.

Koda and the others gathered around, their faces etched with grief as they watched the healer work, their hope fading with each passing hour. Kabota placed a comforting hand on Koda's shoulder, his gaze steady as he met his son's eyes.

"We will honor him, Koda," he said softly. "No matter what happens, Taron's spirit will remain with us. He will guide us, even in death."

As the night wore on, Taron's breathing grew fainter, his strength waning as the pain became too much for his body to bear. He looked up at Omaki, his eyes filled with a mixture of love and regret.

"I am sorry, Omaki," he whispered. "I wanted... to protect you... to protect them all. But I was not strong enough."

Omaki shook her head, her voice choked with emotion. "You have given us everything, Taron. You are our strength, our guide. And you will always be with us."

With a final, shuddering breath, Taron's eyes closed, his body going still, his spirit passing into the forest, leaving his clan behind to carry on his legacy.

26

LOSS

The loss of Taron left a void in the clan, a sense of emptiness that could not be filled. For days, they mourned in silence, their hearts heavy with grief as they struggled to come to terms with his death. Omaki retreated into solitude, her sorrow a quiet, private burden that she carried alone, her heart broken by the loss of her mate.

Koda felt anger and sorrow, a burning desire for justice that gnawed at him, filling him with a sense of purpose he had never felt before. He knew Adanowa was responsible for Taron's death, that the rogue's rage and hatred had driven him to commit an unforgivable act.

But he also knew that revenge would not bring Taron back, that their leader's legacy was one of strength and resilience, not violence and hatred.

Kabota gathered the clan one evening, his voice steady as he spoke, his words filled with both sorrow and hope. "Taron was more than a leader—he was our friend, our family. He gave his life to keep us safe, to ensure that we would survive. And it is our duty to honor his memory, to carry his spirit with us as we move forward."

The clan nodded, their faces solemn as they listened, each feeling the weight of Taron's legacy, the responsibility that now rested on their shoulders.

To honor Taron's memory, the clan held a sacred ceremony, gathering at a hidden glade deep within their territory, a place known only to their kind. It was here that they buried their fallen leader, his body laid to rest beneath a great tree, its branches stretching high into the sky, a symbol of the strength and resilience that Taron had embodied.

Each member of the clan took turns speaking, sharing memories of Taron, stories of his courage and kindness, of the wisdom he had imparted to them. Koda stepped forward, his voice filled with emotion as he spoke of the lessons Taron had taught him, the guidance he had provided, and the strength he had inspired.

As they finished, Omaki stepped forward, her voice trembling with emotion as she placed a hand on Taron's grave. "You are part of this forest now, Taron," she whispered. "Your spirit will live on in the trees, the rivers, the land that you loved. And we will carry you with us, always."

The clan stood in silence, their heads bowed in respect as they paid their final respects, each of them feeling the weight of Taron's presence, a spirit that would guide them, even in death.

Meika, had always been close to her father, her quiet nature a reflection of his own calm wisdom. She spent her days wandering the paths her father had walked, retracing his steps, listening to the sounds of the forest he had loved so deeply. She found solace in the places they had shared, each tree and riverbank a reminder of his presence, a way to keep him close, even as the reality of his absence settled over her.

Meika often sat by the river at dusk, her gaze distant, her thoughts filled with memories of Taron's gentle guidance, his steady voice as he taught her to track and hunt, to respect the life of the forest. She whispered to the trees, her voice a quiet prayer, hoping that her father's spirit would hear her, that he would know how much she missed him, how deeply she felt his absence.

Raela, on the other hand, was filled with confusion and a sense of abandonment she could not put into words. At only ten years old, she struggled to understand the concept of death, the finality of it, the idea that her father would never return. She clung to her mother, seeking comfort in her presence, her mind unable to comprehend why her father had left them.

In the evenings, Raela would sit around, her eyes searching the shadows as if expecting her father to appear, to reassure her that everything would be all right. She asked questions Omaki found diffi-cult to answer, her innocence a painful reminder of the life Taron had been robbed of, the future she would never see.

"I miss him, Mother," Raela whispered one night, her voice carrying a quiet sadness that broke Omaki's heart. "When will he come back?"

Omaki held her close, her heart aching as she struggled to find the words. "He is with us, Raela," she said softly. "He is part of the forest now, watching over us, guiding us. He will always be with you, even if you cannot see him."

Paka mourned in silence, his grief hidden beneath a mask of strength and resolve. He had always admired his father, his heart filled with a fierce loyalty that drove him to prove himself, to live up to the standards he had set. But now, that loyalty had transformed into a need for revenge, a desire to protect his family how his father had.

Paka often practiced his tracking skills, honing his abilities with a determination that bordered on obsession. He spent hours each day following trails, learning the patterns of the forest, preparing himself for the day when he would face Adanowa, when he would have the chance to honor his father's memory by protecting those he had loved.

Each of Taron's children carried their grief in their own way, their lives forever changed by the loss of their father. And as they navigated the darkness of their mourning, they found strength in each other, a bond that would guide them through the challenges that lay ahead.

The ceremony ended as the sun began to set, casting a warm, golden light over the glade. The clan returned to their den sad, yet filled with renewed purpose. They knew they would face challenges ahead, that the forest would test them in ways they could not yet imagine.

But they also knew they were not alone—that Taron's spirit would watch over them, guiding them as they carried on his legacy of strength, unity, and love.

PART III

27

ANGER

Far from the cave of their clan, Erek and Varo had spent the last several months exploring and learning from neighboring clans, immersing themselves in the varied lives and customs of their kind across the peninsula. It was a journey Taron had encouraged them to take, a way to broaden their understanding, deepen their skills, and learn the ways of different clans. But one night, as they sat around with members of the Red Valley Clan, a distant yet familiar call echoed through the trees—a low, mournful sound that tugged at their hearts, stirring a sense of urgency and dread.

It was Omaki's call, a call they recognized instantly, filled with a pain and grief that transcended words. Without hesitation, Erek and Varo left the other clans, driven by an unspoken understanding that something terrible had happened. They moved quickly, their hearts heavy with fear and determination, their minds racing with questions they dared not speak.

They arrived at their clan's cave days later, met by silence. The laughter and conversation were replaced by a somber stillness. Omaki was waiting for them at the edge of the clearing, her face lined with sorrow, her eyes filled with unshed tears.

Erek and Varo approached her, expressions tense, bracing for the worst. "Mother," Erek said. "What happened?"

Omaki looked at them, her gaze steady but filled with a grief that cut through them like a blade. "Your father," she said, her voice breaking. "Taron... He is gone. Adanowa... He took him from us."

It hit them like a storm, and for a moment, neither could speak. Erek clenched his fists, trembling with rage, while Varo's face twisted in pain, his eyes filling with tears. The loss of their father, the pillar of their family, the leader they had looked up to their entire lives, was an unimaginable blow.

Erek took a step forward, his voice shaking with anger. "Where is he? Where is Adanowa? I will end him for what he's done."

Omaki reached out, placing a hand on Erek's shoulder, her touch grounding him, calming the storm that raged within him. "Adanowa will face justice," she said softly. "But you must not act out of anger alone. Revenge will not bring your father back."

But Erek's mind was consumed by the image of his father, lying wounded and helpless in the forest, betrayed by the very creature he had tried to protect his family from. He could feel the anger boiling within him, a need for retribution that would not be silenced. Varo stood beside him, his expression mirroring his brother's, a fierce determination settling over him as he looked toward the forest, his mind filled with thoughts of vengeance.

"Adanowa will pay for this," Varo said quietly. "He will pay for what he has done to our family."

Over the weeks, as Erek and Varo wrestled with their rage, Erek and Varo's anger only grew, their desire for revenge consuming them, driving them to seek out Adanowa, to end the threat to their family. They spent hours training, honing their skills, preparing for the inevitable battle.

Erek took to the forest with a vengeance, tracking every scent, every movement, determined to find any sign of the rogue. He practiced his fighting skills, his muscles hardening as he pushed himself to his limits, his mind focused on a single goal.

Varo, equally driven, used his agility and speed to his advantage, perfecting his ability to move through the forest without a sound, to blend into the shadows, to become a ghost in the trees. He knew that Adanowa was a formidable opponent, that the rogue's strength and cunning would make him a deadly adversary. But he was prepared to face him, to avenge his father's death, no matter the cost.

Together, Erek and Varo planned their approach, each of them contributing their unique skills to the hunt. Erek's strength and endurance would allow him to confront Adanowa head-on, while Varo's speed and stealth would give them the advantage of surprise, the element of unpredictability that could turn the tide in their favor.

Omaki watched her sons with a mixture of pride and sorrow, her heart torn between her desire to protect them and her understanding of their need for justice. She knew that Taron's death had changed them, had forced them to confront the darker aspects of their nature, the anger and pain that simmered beneath the surface.

But she also knew that revenge would not heal their wounds, that it would not bring Taron back or erase the loss they had suffered. And so, she tried to temper their rage, to remind them of the values their father had instilled in them, the importance of balance, of respect for the life of the forest.

"Adanowa is a creature of rage," she said to them one evening, her voice calm but filled with a quiet strength. "He is driven by hatred, by a desire to destroy. But you are not like him. You are your father's sons, guided by honor, by love for your family. Do not let his darkness consume you."

Erek and Varo listened, their expressions thoughtful, their minds filled with a turmoil they could not easily resolve. They understood their mother's words, but the need for justice, for retribution, was a fire that burned within them, a force they could not ignore.

So, with Omaki's blessing, they prepared to confront Adanowa, to seek out the rogue and put an end to his reign of terror. They knew that the journey would be dangerous, that the fight would test them in ways they could not yet imagine. But they were ready, their hearts filled with a determination that could not be shaken.

28

DEPARTURE

In the days leading up to their departure, the clan rallied around Erek and Varo, offering their support, their skills, their wisdom. Kabota took them aside, his voice steady as he imparted the knowledge he had gained from his own battles, his experience a valuable asset in the fight ahead.

"You are strong, both of you," he said, his gaze steady as he looked at them. "But strength alone will not be enough. You must be smart, cautious, aware of every movement, every sound. Adanowa is cunning, and he will exploit any weakness. Trust each other, rely on your bond as brothers. Together, you are unstoppable."

Koda watched his brothers with admiration and fear, his heart heavy with the knowledge that they were risking their lives, that the outcome of their confrontation was uncertain. He wanted to join them, to fight alongside them, but he knew that his time would come, that he still had much to learn.

The younger siblings, too, gathered around Erek and Varo, each offering their own form of support, a silent promise to carry on their father's legacy, to protect their family, no matter the cost.

As the day of their departure approached, Omaki gathered the clan for a final farewell, her voice filled with a quiet resolve as she spoke, her words a reminder of the bond that held them together.

"We are more than a family," she said, her gaze sweeping over each of them. "We are a part of this forest, a force of nature, guided by the strength and wisdom of those who came before us. Erek, Varo, you are the sons of Taron, and his spirit will guide you, protect you. Go with courage, with honor. And remember—you are never alone."

With those words, Erek and Varo set out, their minds focused on their task. They knew that the journey ahead would be difficult, that the fight with Adanowa would test them in ways they could not yet imagine. But they were ready, their bond as brothers, as sons of Taron, a force that would drive them forward, a light in the darkness of their grief.

And as they disappeared into the forest, their family watched, their hearts filled with both pride and sorrow, a silent prayer following them, a hope that they would return, victorious, their father's legacy upheld, their family whole once more.

29

UNITY

In the days following Erek and Varo's vow to avenge their father, Kabota found himself torn between loyalty to his late friend and the fierce protective instincts he felt toward his family. He had known Taron well enough, had fought beside him, laughed with him, and built a bond that went beyond words. He knew Taron would never have wanted his sons to throw themselves into danger for the sake of revenge. But Kabota also understood the depth of Erek and Varo's grief, the fire that burned within them to protect the clan from the ever-present threat of Adanowa.

For Kabota, this wasn't simply about vengeance—it was about survival. Adanowa's unpredictable attacks, his looming presence on the borders of their territory, and his unyielding hostility had turned their peaceful existence into a landscape of constant vigilance and fear. Kabota could see the strain it put on the clan, the way it affected their daily lives, how even the younger ones moved through the forest with a quiet wariness, their innocence overshadowed by the threat of violence.

One night, as the clan slept, Kabota sat alone on a ledge overlooking the forest, his mind racing with memories of Taron and the unspoken promise they had shared to protect their families at all costs. He knew Taron had been driven by a fierce love for his family, a devotion that had kept him grounded, even in the face of adversity. And Kabota realized that he, too, was driven by that same love, that same need to protect his family.

In his heart, he knew what he had to do. He would join Erek and Varo, not out of a desire for vengeance, but out of duty to his clan, to ensure the legacy Taron left behind would continue, that his family would be safe and free from the shadow of Adanowa's rage.

As dawn broke over the forest, Kabota approached Erek and Varo, his expression calm but resolute. "When the time comes, I will be with you," he said, his voice steady. "Your father would want us to protect this clan, to bring peace back to our lives. But we must be smart, strategic. Adanowa is cunning, and we cannot let anger cloud our judgment."

Erek and Varo exchanged a glance, a flicker of surprise crossing their faces. They had not expected Kabota to join them, but his words filled them with a renewed sense of purpose, a reminder that this mission was about more than vengeance—it was about honor, about protecting the family Taron had devoted his life to.

The forest was heavy with silence as Kabota, Erek, and Varo prepared to confront Adanowa, each braced for battle. They had spent days planning every step, every movement, each resolved to bring an end to the threat Adanowa posed to their family. But as they made their way deeper into the woods, an unspoken question lingered between them: Was vengeance truly what Taron would have wanted? Would the spirit of their father, a leader who had valued peace and unity above all else, have wanted his sons to carry on his legacy with violence?

Kabota, aware of the turmoil in Erek and Varo, paused, then in a low, thoughtful voice said, "Your father sought peace whenever he could, even in times of great conflict. Taron always believed there was a way forward without bloodshed. If there is a chance to end this without taking his life... I think he would have wanted us to consider it."

Erek and Varo exchanged a look as they absorbed Kabota's words.

Both carried a deep-seated anger toward Adanowa, a rage that had driven them to seek revenge. But they also knew their father had been a creature of compassion and understanding, a leader who had guided his family with wisdom and restraint.

After a long silence, Varo nodded. "Then we will do this for him. We will give Adanowa a choice—a chance to end this."

Kabota nodded as he watched the two brothers come to an agreement, their commitment to honoring their father's legacy outweighing their desire for revenge. Together, they sent a series of deep, resonant calls through the forest, a summons that would draw Adanowa to them.

30

BATTLE

They waited in silence, the forest around them alive with tension as they listened for any sign of Adanowa's approach. Their calls echoed through the trees, a sound both challenging and beckoning, a message that could not be ignored.

After a few tense moments, a low growl reached their ears, a sound filled with hostility and anger. Adanowa stepped into the clearing, his massive form casting a long shadow as he approached, his eyes gleaming with malice.

"Kabota," he sneered, his voice dripping with contempt. "You think you can summon me like a creature to be tamed? I am no servant, no follower. I am a force unto myself."

Kabota held his ground, his voice calm but firm. "We called you here to give you a choice, Adanowa. This can end peacefully, without bloodshed. We are giving you the chance to walk away."

Adanowa let out a harsh laugh, his expression twisted with scorn. "Peace? There is no peace in this forest, Kabota. There is only power, only the strong and the weak. And I do not answer to the weak."

With a roar, Adanowa lunged, his massive body hurtling toward them with a force that shook the ground. Kabota, Erek, and Varo moved in unison, their years of training and experience guiding their actions as they dodged his attack, each of them focused and precise.

Adanowa fought with brutal strength, his movements wild and relentless, each blow bone-jarring. But Kabota and the brothers held their ground, working together to evade his attacks, wearing him down with every pass. They struck in coordinated movements, targeting his flanks, his legs, each blow weakening his resolve, forcing him to expend more and more energy.

As the battle wore on, Adanowa's movements grew slower, his breath labored, his body marked by the strain of the confrontation. He was powerful but alone, and the unity of Kabota, Erek, and Varo gave them an advantage he could not overcome.

In a final, desperate attempt, Adanowa lunged at Kabota, claws outstretched, face twisted with hatred. But Kabota sidestepped, his movements calm and controlled, his eyes filled with quiet determination. He reached out, catching Adanowa's arm, and with a swift, practiced motion, he brought the rogue to the ground, pinning him with a strength that left Adanowa struggling in vain.

Erek and Varo moved to stand beside him, their expressions filled with anger and sorrow as they looked down at the creature who had taken so much from them.

"We could end this now," Varo said. "We could put an end to his threat, once and for all."

Kabota tightened his grip, his gaze steady as he looked into Adanowa's eyes, seeing the hatred, the pain, the years of anger that had twisted him into the creature he had become. "No, Varo," he said softly. "We will not kill him. We are not like him."

Adanowa snarled, his voice filled with bitterness. "Spare me your pity, Kabota. I am no charity case. If you will not end me, then let me go, and I will return as I always have."

But Kabota shook his head, his voice calm but resolute. "You have a choice, Adanowa. You can continue this path, continue the life of rage and solitude, or you can choose a different way. You can choose to walk a path of peace, to stop living as a creature of darkness."

For a long moment, Adanowa was silent, his gaze filled with a mixture of anger and confusion. He had never been offered mercy, never been given a choice beyond survival and vengeance. The concept of peace, of community, was foreign to him, a notion he had long abandoned.

Without another word, Kabota released him, stepping back as he watched Adanowa rise to his feet, his body tense. The rogue looked at them, his expression unreadable, his mind wrestling with the unexpected choice they had given him.

He turned and disappeared into the forest, leaving Kabota, Erek, and Varo to wonder if they had made the right decision.

31

DOUBT

Erek and Varo wrestled with their decision, their minds filled with doubts and questions that refused to be silenced. Sparing Adanowa had been a choice guided by honor, by the desire to honor their father's memory. But the uncertainty, the fear that they had allowed a threat to continue, weighed heavily on them.

Erek often found himself retracing the steps they had taken, questioning whether mercy had been the right path, whether sparing Adanowa had been a mistake. He would sit by the river, his gaze distant, his thoughts filled with memories of Taron and the quiet strength he had embodied.

"Father would have wanted peace," he said to himself, his voice filled with sadness and determination. "He would have wanted us to give Adanowa a chance, even if it seems impossible."

Varo, too, struggled with the decision, his mind filled with thoughts of revenge, of the satisfaction that taking Adanowa's life might have brought. But he remembered his father's words, the lessons Taron had taught him about honor, about choosing a path that would protect the clan, not one that would fill their lives with more violence. Together, the two brothers found solace knowing they had done what Taron would have wanted, that they had honored his memory by choosing mercy over vengeance. But the lingering fear, the uncertainty of Adanowa's intentions, remained a shadow that would take time to dissipate.

32

GIFT

As the weeks passed, the clan settled back into their routines, their lives slowly returning to a semblance of normalcy. But one morning, as they awoke to begin their day, they found an unusual sight waiting for them at the edge of the clearing—a small bundle of berries, roots, and herbs, carefully arranged.

Omaki's eyes narrowed as she examined the bundle. "Who would leave such a gift? These are not the kind of offerings left by neighboring clans."

Kabota approached, his expression thoughtful as he recognized the signs. "It was Adanowa. He must have left these for us."

The clan exchanged uncertain glances, their hearts filled with fear and hope. The idea that Adanowa, the creature who had once threatened their clan, would leave a gift was almost inconceivable. Yet here it was, a sign that perhaps their act of mercy had sparked something within him, a glimmer of change.

Over the next few weeks, similar gifts appeared at the edge of the clearing—berries, roots, even a large deer kill. Each offering was a gesture, a silent acknowledgment of the mercy they had shown him, a sign that Adanowa was reaching out, attempting to bridge the divide that had separated him from them.

Omaki was cautious, her heart wary as she considered the implications. She remembered the pain Adanowa had caused, the life he had taken, the grief that had torn through their family. But she also understood the power of redemption, the strength it took to change, to seek a new path.

Kabota, too, was cautious but hopeful, his heart filled with quiet satisfaction as he watched the rogue's transformation unfold. He knew Taron would have wanted this, would have seen the possibility for change, for healing, even in the darkest of souls.

For Erek and Varo, the journey was more difficult, their minds filled with conflicting emotions as they tried to reconcile the creature who had taken their father's life with the one who now sought to make amends. They struggled to let go of their anger, their grief, to see Adanowa not as an enemy but as a creature capable of change.

33

PERSISTENCE

As the months passed, Adanowa's gestures grew more frequent, his presence a quiet, almost ghostly figure who lingered on the edges of their territory, observing from a distance, never encroaching but always near. The clan grew used to his presence, their initial fear and suspicion slowly giving way to a cautious acceptance. One evening, as the sun set over the forest, Adanowa approached the clearing, his steps slow, his gaze filled with a mixture of uncertainty and humility. He looked at the clan, his eyes searching, as if seeking permission to come closer. Omaki, her heart filled with a strange sense of peace, stepped forward, her voice calm but welcoming. "You may come closer, Adanowa. If you truly wish to join us, we will not turn you away." He hesitated, his expression unreadable. But after a long silence, he nodded, his gaze filled with a mixture of gratitude and relief as he took a tentative step forward, his form blending with the shadows as he joined the clan.

In the days that followed, Adanowa slowly integrated into their lives, his presence a quiet but steady reminder of the power of forgiveness, of the strength it took to change. The clan watched him with caution, curiosity, and hope that perhaps, after all they had endured, there was a path to peace. Erek and Varo, though still grappling with their own grief, found solace in the knowledge that they had honored their father's legacy, that they had chosen a path of mercy, a path that would bring healing rather than more pain.

And as the forest blossomed with new life, as the trees filled with the sounds of spring, the clan found peace in the unity they had forged, in the knowledge that they had given even the darkest soul a chance to find redemption. They had chosen a path that would carry them forward, bound not by anger, but by love, by forgiveness, by the unbreakable bond that held them together, a family that would endure, a family that would thrive.

34

APPEAL

The sun barely touched the eastern horizon when Adanowa found himself standing at the edge of the clan's quiet encampment, his eyes scanning the misted treetops. He felt the gravity of his task ahead—making amends with each member of the clan. Every step he took seemed weighted by his past, yet he was resolute to earn their acceptance. He looked around and spotted Omaki first, already awake and tending to a task near the river.

Omaki had always been the keeper of knowledge within the clan. Her wisdom guided them through conflicts and conundrums, and her distrust of Adanowa was as rooted as the ancient trees surrounding them. He approached her slowly, hands visible, in a posture of openness.

"Omaki," he began, voice low, "I know you doubt my intentions. My past is full of mistakes, but I hope you'll allow me a chance to prove that I can be different."

Omaki paused, barely acknowledging him. Her face was stern, eyes sharp as they darted from her task to Adanowa. "Words are easy, Adanowa. Your actions will show if you are worthy of our trust."

Taking Omaki's silent challenge to heart, Adanowa returned every morning to assist her, learning the delicate rituals of herb gathering, understanding their medicinal purposes, and the stories behind each plant. With each shared task, Omaki began to speak to him—at first curtly, and then gradually with instruction and, perhaps, a tinge of respect.

Adanowa turned his attention to Meika next. She had been among the loudest critics when he was first brought back, her voice ringing with condemnation. If he was to gain her trust, he would need to demonstrate his dedication to the safety of the clan in ways she could not ignore.

He began following her as she scouted the forest, always keeping a respectful distance. Meika pretended not to notice at first, her movements quick and precise as she navigated the dense terrain, marking trails, and noting signs of danger. But Adanowa was determined. He studied her methods silently, observing how she moved, the way she read the forest like an open book.

Over time, his presence became harder to ignore. One day, as she crouched beside a trail of disturbed leaves, Meika glanced over her shoulder at him. "If you're going to shadow me, you might as well make yourself useful," she said, her tone sharp but not unkind.

Adanowa nodded, stepping forward with purpose. Meika was skilled, but he could see the gaps in her knowledge—the places where her instincts were sharp but her techniques could be refined. Rather than simply following her lead, Adanowa began offering subtle guidance, pointing out things she might have missed: the faint scent of a predator on the wind, the nearly imperceptible tilt of a broken twig, or the way moss grew heavier on one side of a tree, hinting at direction.

At first, Meika bristled at his input, her pride flaring. "I've been scouting these woods my whole life," she snapped one afternoon after he corrected her misinterpretation of a trail.

Adanowa didn't flinch. "And I've been surviving them in ways you've never needed to," he replied calmly, his voice low but firm. "Let me show you what I've learned."

Despite her irritation, curiosity tugged at her resolve. She began to watch him more closely, paying attention as he demonstrated how to blend with the forest, his steps leaving barely a trace. He showed her how to distinguish the tracks of a frightened deer from one merely grazing and how to recognize the signs of human presence long before they became a threat.

Over time, their dynamic shifted. Meika's initial wariness gave way to reluctant respect as she began to grasp the depth of his knowledge. One evening, as the forest grew quiet under the fading light of dusk, Meika finally stopped and turned to face him.

"You're better at this than I expected," she admitted grudgingly, her tone laced with both admiration and defiance. "But that doesn't mean I trust you."

Adanowa met her eyes. "I'm not asking for your trust," he said. "Only that you use what I've taught you to protect the clan."

Meika hesitated before giving a sharp nod. Though her words still carried the edge of caution, the forest had become their common ground. In their shared work and the unspoken understanding of the dangers they faced, a fragile connection began to grow—built not on trust, but on the mutual goal of keeping their clan safe.

The young ones, Raela and Paka, had always been wary of him, eyes wide with uncertainty whenever he was near. Adanowa knew he had to tread carefully with them. They were innocent, untouched by the betrayals of the past, and he wanted to give them no reason to fear him.

He began by bringing them small gifts he found during his walks —an unusual feather, a bright stone, sometimes even a snippet of a story. Slowly, they warmed to him. Paka would run to him in the mornings, excited to see what trinket he had found, while Raela would silently observe from a distance, a look of cautious curiosity in her eyes.

One evening, Adanowa taught them a small game he had learned as a little one, a game of strategy and wit involving stones and sticks. The laughter that followed felt like a balm to his soul. It was in those moments that he felt something genuine—a fragile but real connection forming between him and the clan's future generation.

But Koda was different. He had watched Adanowa from the

beginning, his emotions shifting between distrust and a hesitant curiosity that he kept buried deep within. For Koda, Adanowa's presence was an open wound—a painful reminder of past betrayals and a danger to the delicate balance of his feelings.

The tension between them simmered beneath every interaction. Koda's heart was a tangled mess of suspicion and an inexplicable pull toward this stranger who had, for some reason, chosen redemption over escape. He found himself torn, watching Adanowa form connections with the clan, unsure whether to feel threatened or relieved.

One night, Koda approached Adanowa as he sat alone, gazing at the stars.

"Why do you stay?" Koda's voice was rough, betraying the turmoil within him.

Adanowa didn't look away from the stars. "Because I need to. For you, for the clan, and... for myself. Running would mean accepting that I'm still that beast you all remember. Staying means I get to try and change that."

Koda's silence spoke volumes, a tentative truce taking root in the quiet.

35

MACHINES

Just as fragile bonds began to form, a new threat emerged. The clan had sensed human encroachment for months now—the scent of foreign metals, the faint hum of machinery disrupting the silence of their territory. But now, it had escalated. Human drones buzzed through the forest, a sharp mechanical contrast to the natural harmony of the wilderness.

The clan had been discussing ways to avoid detection. Adanowa offered his knowledge, describing the humans' predictable scouting patterns, the best times to evade them, and the paths they would likely avoid.

Koda, however, even at his young age, felt the oppressive weight of responsibility. He volunteered to scout the perimeter, insisting on ensuring the safety of the clan. Adanowa offered to go with him, but Koda declined, wary of the humans' reaction if they spotted them together. Adanowa reluctantly stayed behind, tension lacing every muscle as he watched Koda disappear into the trees.

The morning was still when Koda caught sight of the drone, its sleek body slicing through the forest air, blinking lights scanning for movement. He froze, breath shallow, watching it hover dangerously close to his position. He crouched lower, moving silently between the trees, but the drone had caught sight of him.

Koda dashed, weaving through the underbrush, but the mechanical whir followed, relentless in its pursuit. A second later, he heard human voices, boots crunching on the forest floor.

"Sector B has movement. All units, proceed with caution."

Koda's pulse quickened, fear sharpening his instincts. He darted between shadows, his ears straining to pinpoint the direction of the encroaching humans. He had no choice but to keep moving, each step a calculated risk.

Just when he thought he was cornered, a voice called out with a deep guttural howl in the distance, drawing the humans' attention away.

"Over here! Movement spotted near the ridge." Adanowa's voice echoed through the trees, a loud and unmistakable lure.

Koda watched in shock as the humans turned, following Adanowa's voice as he led them deeper into the woods. The moment he had the chance, Koda moved, slipping out of sight and making his way back to the clan's territory. He didn't stop until he was safely beyond their reach, his chest heaving as he turned to see Adanowa reappear, cautious but unharmed.

"You saved me," Koda said, breathless.

Adanowa's expression was hard to read, a mixture of relief and something deeper. "We're clan," he replied simply.

When they returned, the clan listened as Koda recounted the encounter, a new layer of respect coloring his words. For the first time, he spoke of Adanowa's actions without suspicion clouding his voice.

The next day, Omaki addressed Adanowa before the entire clan, her tone less severe, carrying an unexpected gentleness.

"You have shown us your intentions, Adanowa. You risked your life for one of ours. That is no small thing."

Meika nodded, her arms crossed, yet a glimmer of pride flickered in her eyes. Even Raela and Paka watched him with newfound admiration.

Koda, standing beside him, placed a hand on Adanowa's shoulder. It was a gesture of solidarity, an unspoken acknowledgment of the bond they now shared.

Despite the clan's cautious acceptance, the threat of human encroachment loomed larger than ever. The drones had proven relentless, and the humans' tactics were becoming increasingly invasive. Adanowa knew they needed a plan to protect their home.

Over the following weeks, he and Kabota worked together, often deep into the night, mapping out safe routes, discussing tactics, and learning each other's strengths and weaknesses. A bond grew, shaped by shared purpose and trust forged in the fires of survival.

As the clan huddled one evening, Adanowa looked at the faces around him, feeling the warmth of belonging. For the first time in a long time, he was not just surviving—he was part of something greater than himself. He had found a family, one willing to give him a chance, however hard-won.

And though the threat of the humans continued to press against their borders, Adanowa knew he would stand with them, whatever may come. The bonds he had forged were now his to protect, his past no longer a burden but a foundation for the future he was building, one step at a time.

36

TRADITION

As summer's warmth settled over the peninsula, the clan buzzed with tension. The annual elk hunt was upon them, an ancient tradition that united all the forest clans for weeks of ritual, skill, and survival. It was a time for strengthening alliances and honoring the spirits of the wild, a time for old rivalries to simmer and, sometimes, new conflicts to ignite.

For the clan of Adanowa, this year's hunt carried a weight of its own. The choice to let Adanowa live—and, more controversially, join their ranks—would soon be scrutinized by all the clans. Rumors about Taron's death had already spread, tangled with whispers of betrayal, strength, and justice. They would face the reactions of the other clans for the first time, and no one knew how they would be received.

The morning light was barely breaking over the treetops when Asha and Kabota called the clan together. They gathered in the clearing, the air heavy with anticipation. Asha stepped forward, her calm, assured presence a balm against the swirling doubts among her kin.

"Tomorrow, we join the other clans," she began, her voice steady. "They will have questions—about Taron, about Adanowa. Some may greet us with respect, others with hostility. But we stand together."

Kabota, took his place beside his mate. "We chose to give Adanowa a chance because we saw something in him. They may not understand, but we do. We must show them our resolve."

Adanowa listened from the edge of the group, his face a mix of gratitude and apprehension. He knew the clan was risking their reputation, even their safety, by standing with him. As he met Kabota's gaze, he saw no resentment—only determination.

With the decision made, the clan moved as one to prepare for the journey. They wove charms from pine needles and mountain sage to keep their spirits strong.

Omaki prepared healing herbs, her hands moving with practiced ease as she explained to Adanowa the significance of each one. "These aren't just for wounds of the flesh," she told him, pressing a small pouch into his hand. "They're for wounds of the heart and spirit. You may need them."

By nightfall, the clan was ready. Their cave lay silent under the stars, each member of the clan deep in thought as they anticipated the next day's journey.

At dawn, they set out. The other clans had already begun to arrive, each group marked by the colors and symbols of their own heritage. The gathering grounds were alive with familiar faces—old allies, respected rivals, and curious onlookers all mingling in the open fields and forested edges.

As Asha and Kabota led their group forward, whispers rose among the other clans. Eyes flickered over Adanowa, some filled with hostility, others with a wary curiosity. The weight of those gazes made the air thick, each step forward an act of defiance.

Their clan soon found a place to set up camp at the edge of the gathering grounds. The other clans were spread out nearby. As the afternoon sun dipped low, casting long shadows through the trees, a group from the Stone Ridge Clan approached, led by Jarok. His gaze was sharp and unyielding, moving over each member of the clan before stopping on Adanowa, who stood at the back of the group.

"So," Jarok began, his voice a low rumble, "the rumors were true. Taron was killed. And you spared his killer?" His words were directed toward Kabota, whose expression remained firm as he faced the elder.

"We chose to spare him because we saw his desire to change," Kabota replied, his voice steady and unwavering. "Adanowa fights alongside us now."

Jarok's gaze narrowed, his hand flexing at his side as he considered Kabota's response. "Perhaps your clan is wiser than we give you credit for," he said, though his tone carried an edge of doubt. "But mark my words—if he fails, it will be on all your heads." The warning hung in the air as Jarok gave Adanowa a final, hard look before retreating back toward his clan's encampment. Kabota's stance didn't falter, but the atmosphere was heavy with the weight of his words.

Throughout the day, delegations from other clans approached, each reacting to Adanowa's presence in their own way. The Red Valley Clan, led by Marla, arrived with a mix of respect and quiet disapproval, their members glancing warily in Adanowa's direction. Some clan members whispered to one another, skeptical of the clan's decision, while a few looked on with admiration, impressed by the courage it took to give someone like Adanowa a second chance.

However, members of Taron's old allies were far less forgiving. The Riverbend Clan, led by Tyrek, approached Omaki with a cold, reproachful demeanor. Tyrek's expression was severe, his gaze piercing as he addressed her.

"We heard what happened to Taron," he said, his voice barely concealing his anger. "The one who killed him walks free?"

Omaki met his gaze with unwavering calm. "Taron was respected, yes, but not infallible. We all knew he harbored grudges, but he also believed in second chances. We chose to give Adanowa a path to redemption."

Tyrek's eyes flickered, his frown deepening. "Perhaps. But for many, Taron was a friend. Seeing his killer here, standing among you, will not sit well with them."

Varo stood nearby watching closely. Tension lay beneath his stoic expression. He and Tyrek exchanged a brief look, acknowledging the difficult decision the clan had made and the risks they now faced.

Despite the tense exchanges, the bonds of tradition held—no one dared to challenge the clan directly, not yet.

As evening approached, mist shrouded the gathering ground, and a chill settled over the clans as they prepared for the night. Adanowa found himself walking near the edge of the camp when he was confronted by a small group from the Mistwood Clan, led by Lora, a fierce warrior known for her sharp instincts. Beside her was Rivak, Taron's younger brother, his face a mask of grief and barely contained anger.

"You think you can walk here like one of us?" Rivak spat, stepping closer to Adanowa, his voice laced with vitriol "Taron deserved better than to be cut down by a traitor." Adanowa held his ground, his face solemn as he prepared to respond, but Erek stepped forward before he could speak, placing a firm hand on Rivak's shoulder. "We mourn Taron, my father too," Erek said, his voice calm but steely. "But this was our choice, and we will answer for it if need be."

Rivak's glare softened as he looked at Erek, though the bitterness in his eyes remained. After a moment, he nodded stiffly, stepping back with one final, contemptuous look in Adanowa's direction. The encounter left an uneasy silence in the air, a reminder of the fragile acceptance Adanowa had yet to fully earn.

With the arrival of dusk, the clans gathered in a large circle at the heart of the gathering grounds. Each clan leader stepped forward to offer blessings to the spirits of the forest, their voices rising in prayer and song, a tradition that had been passed down through generations.

Adanowa stood on the outskirts of his clan's group, aware of the eyes on him as Kabota stepped forward to offer their clan's prayers. Kabota's voice was deep and steady, calling upon the spirits for guidance, strength, and protection. As he spoke, the weight of the other clans' stares pressed on Adanowa, each a reminder that his presence was tolerated but not accepted.

In the silence that followed, the leaders gave the signal, and the hunt began.

Adanowa, with Erek and Varo, set off into the dense forest, their movements synchronized and silent. The earlier tension hung over them like a storm cloud, but the thrill of the hunt took precedence. Tracking the elk required precision, patience, and trust—qualities that each clan prided themselves on and valued in others.

Yet as they moved deeper into the woods, Adanowa's thoughts drifted back to the gathering grounds, to the looks of mistrust and resentment. His presence among them was tenuous, and in the quiet moments between footfalls, he wondered if he would ever truly belong.

Several days passed, the hunt progressing with each clan carving out their own territory within the forest. Each evening, the clans regrouped to share news, strategies, and stories, but every interaction was layered with unspoken tension. On the third day, as Adanowa ventured farther into the hunting grounds alone, he sensed someone watching him. Moments later, he saw Rivak standing among the trees, his posture rigid, his eyes glinting with anger. "Some of us have not forgotten what you did," Rivak sneered, his voice low and filled with menace. "Remember that, Adanowa. The forest holds its memories as well as we do."

Adanowa met Rivak's gaze, his expression steady, and gave a slight nod, choosing silence over confrontation. He understood their hatred, perhaps even accepted it as part of his redemption. But he would not falter, and he would continue to prove himself, even if it took the rest of his life.

As the days wore on, the clans began to notice strange disturbances along the edges of their hunting grounds. Drone-like noises would occasionally hum through the forest, and some had seen flashes of movement, pale glimpses of humans venturing farther into the woods than ever before.

One evening, Asha gathered the clan to discuss the threat. "We have all sensed the humans are closer this year. We must tread carefully." Kabota took her lead, his face hard with worry. "They search more desperately now, and if we're found, we risk our sacred gathering grounds." The clan nodded in agreement, all aware of the humans' relentless encroachment. Adanowa listened intently, knowing that his knowledge of the humans could prove useful. Quietly, he offered his insight, suggesting routes and hiding places to help avoid detection. Though some still eyed him with suspicion, his advice was taken, and that night they slept with a renewed sense of caution.

As the sun set on the final day of the hunt, the clan gathered once more. They had faced mistrust, old resentments, and the dangers of the outside world. But through it all, they had also found something stronger—a unity bound by forgiveness, trust, and the quiet strength of shared struggles.

Adanowa stood among them, not as an outsider but as a member of the clan. And though his journey was far from over, he knew that for the first time, he was not walking it alone. The forest around them breathed a collective sigh, welcoming the peace that the clan had fought so hard to protect, if only for a moment longer.

37

REFLECTION

The Great Hunt had come to an end. Shadows of the early dawn clung to the forest as Erek and Varo walked in silence, reflecting on the triumph of the hunt and the subtle shift in their paths. Their decision to stay behind had loomed in both their minds, and now, as the others packed and prepared to leave, they stole a moment together on a ledge overlooking the valley.

Erek stood on the outcrop fixed on the valley below. The fog hung low, softening the edges of the landscape. He sensed Varo's presence beside him, both lost in thought as they processed the end of the hunt. There was victory in the hunt, certainly, but a strange melancholy had settled in Erek's chest. "It's strange, isn't it?" Erek broke the silence. "Everyone else talks about heading back as though that cave is the only home they'll ever have. Yet, we're here, talking about staying."

Varo gave a quiet chuckle. "Maybe we're both mad." He exhaled deeply. "But something about Stone Ridge... It's different from anywhere I've been. And then there's... well, Kora."

Erek nodded, a knowing smile tugging at the corner of his mouth. "Kora from Stone Ridge and you—who would have thought?" He turned his gaze back to the valley, his thoughts drifting toward Rina, the Riverbend healer whose laughter had lingered in his mind long after he left her clan. Their conversations had been brief but transformative. Rina, with her calm assurance and skilled hands, seemed to understand Erek's inner turmoil in a way no one else had.

"Rina's why you're staying, isn't she?" Varo said, as if reading Erek's mind.

Erek shrugged. "Partly. There's something about her. She speaks of life and the land as though they're part of her. I feel... anchored when I'm around her."

Their decision to remain in the valley was more than personal interest in these females, though that certainly weighed on their hearts. It was also a realization that they had different desires for their futures. The idea of journeying back to the same routines, the same landscapes, felt limiting. They wanted something more, a chance to build lives that had meaning beyond the rhythms of the clan's cycle.

"We're different, Varo," Erek continued, as though convincing himself. "What we want—it's here."

Morning broke slowly over the valley as Omaki, Asha, Kabota, Koda, Meika, Raela, and Paka gathered their things for the journey home. Spirits were high after the hunt, and talk of returning to the cave filled the air, each of them imagining the comfort of home.

"Hard to believe the hunt's over already," Raela said, shouldering her pack. "I'll miss this place a little, but I'll be glad to sleep in my own spot."

Kabota grinned. "Nothing like the feel of the cave walls around you, the familiar smells. Let's get moving. I'd like to make it back by sundown."

They laughed and joked, casting occasional glances around, each noting Erek and Varo's absence with curiosity and unease.

"Strange, isn't it?" Paka said to Asha. "Leaving them here like this."

Asha shrugged, her expression pensive. "They've got reasons, I suppose. Who am I to question them? They're both good hunters, and they know the land well enough to survive."

Omaki, turned toward them, her voice carrying a note of authority that silenced the chatter. "Erek and Varo are making their choice. Our duty is to return to our home. If they choose to come back, they will."

The group nodded, trusting Omaki's words, and they set off toward the path that led back to the cave. As they moved through the forest, the beauty of their surroundings seemed more vivid, as though every leaf, every bird's song, was bidding them farewell. They walked with purpose, each member silently anticipating the stories they would share, and the comfort of home. Yet, in each heart lay a hint of doubt—a quiet, unspoken fear that they were leaving something important behind.

As the group trekked back to the cave, Erek and Varo passed into the heart of Stone Ridge territory, the familiarity of the surroundings no longer foreign but embraced with newfound affection. The clear, crisp air carried scents of pine and wildflowers, guiding them to the central clearing where members of the Stone Ridge and Riverbend clans mingled.

Kora waited, her gaze brightening when she spotted Varo. Her presence was a beacon for him, grounding him and amplifying the decision he'd made to stay.

"Varo," she greeted, her smile unwavering. "Back so soon?"

Varo grinned, a playful light in his eyes. "Couldn't resist. Besides, I had something important to tell you."

Erek left them to their quiet conversation and continued toward the Riverbend side of the clearing, where Rina was teaching a group herbal techniques. Her gentle authority and the way she captivated the others reminded him of why he was here. The kinship they shared was quiet, built on moments that didn't need words.

Rina glanced up, her face softening at the sight of him. "Erek," she called, beckoning him over. "Are you here to stay this time?"

Her question was laced with humor, but he saw the deeper meaning behind her eyes.

"Only if you'll have me," he replied, feeling a rush of gratitude that he didn't have to explain himself further. With Rina, his choice seemed to require no justification; it was simply accepted, woven into the fabric of the lives they had begun to intertwine.

They spoke of plans and dreams, a future that might include more than simply surviving and hunting. In these clans, he and Varo had found not just companionship but a glimpse of purpose—a chance to build, to create, to expand beyond what they had once known.

38

VIOLATION

The sun hung low in the sky as Omaki, Asha, Kabota, Koda, and the rest of the younger members of the clan wound steadily along the forest path. Their trek home had mostly been quiet, each of them drifting into their thoughts, tired but pleased with the outcome of the Great Hunt. Yet, as they approached familiar territory, a strange discomfort settled over them, barely perceptible but persistent, like the distant hum of an oncoming storm.

Kabota was the first to voice what they were all feeling. "Anyone else feel that?" he said, glancing around with a frown. "Something's... off."

Meika nodded, her gaze darting through the thickening trees as they neared the ravine that would lead them to their cave. "It's quiet —too quiet.

Omaki stayed silent as she took in their surroundings. She couldn't shake the prickling sensation on the back of her neck, a primal alertness that had saved her countless times in the past. She motioned for the others to slow down, and they closed ranks, instinctively tightening their formation.

As they crossed the next rise, a faint, pungent odor met their noses, a smell that was both foreign and deeply unsettling. Asha wrinkled her nose, glancing at the others with a look of uncertainty.

"Is that... smoke?" she asked.

Omaki nodded slowly, her expression hardening. "Yes, but this has the stench of chemicals. It's human-made."

A ripple of dread passed through the group as Omaki's words sank in. Their cave, their sanctuary, was well hidden, secured in an isolated part of the valley. The thought of humans being close enough to leave such a scent was unimaginable. With a silent nod from Omaki, they moved forward, their steps cautious, senses heightened. The journey became a tense silence, broken only by the occasional rustling of leaves or the soft crunch of twigs beneath their feet. It was as if the forest itself was holding its breath.

Paka, usually the first to laugh and joke, kept his gaze fixed on the ground, each step measured as though he feared what he might find. "They couldn't have found it, right?" he whispered, almost to himself. "The cave is too hidden, isn't it?"

Koda tried to reassure him. "We've kept it safe, Paka. Maybe it's nothing."

But even his words sounded hollow. As they approached the final stretch, where the last line of dense brush and rocks shielded their home, they all halted in unison, their breaths catching. The trail before them showed signs of recent disturbance—footprints, oddly deep and uneven, like they had been left by someone unaccustomed to the forest terrain.

Raela knelt, her fingers tracing the outline of one of the prints. "They were here," she whispered, her voice a mixture of shock and disbelief. "More than one."

Omaki examined the tracks. "Not just passing through," she said, her voice edged with steel. "They were searching. There's no reason they'd come this close unless they were looking for something."

This was no random intrusion—these humans had come with intent, and they were dangerously close to finding what they sought.

"Let's keep moving," Omaki ordered, her tone brooking no argument. "We need to see if the cave is safe."

With renewed urgency, they pushed forward, hearts pounding as they approached the final bend. But as they rounded the corner, a sight met their eyes that stole the breath from their lungs.

Just outside the mouth of the cave, the ground was scattered with broken branches and trampled earth, as if a small crowd had gathered here. The familiar markers they had used to disguise the entrance—the clusters of rocks and dense shrubbery—had been disturbed, uprooted, and tossed aside. They were small details, but in the silence of the forest, the effect was like a shout.

Koda swallowed hard. "They found it."

Omaki's jaw clenched as she surveyed the area. A chill settled over her, a mixture of anger and helplessness she hadn't felt since Taron's death. Their home, the one place that had always been a sanctuary, had been touched by outsiders. The deep tracks, the shredded branches, even small bits of strange, shiny metal left behind—they were signs of human presence.

Omaki stepped forward, crouching to pick up a fragment of the shiny metal, examining it with a frown. She turned it over in her hand, feeling the strange, cold weight. Humans left traces of their presence wherever they went, and this metal shard felt like an invasion of more than just their physical space; it was an intrusion upon the heart of the clan.

Raela let out a quiet gasp. "If they've been here... If they know about the cave, we can't stay. It's too dangerous."

Omaki nodded, though the decision weighed heavily upon her. "We'll have to leave. But we won't do it without careful planning."

The clan members exchanged glances, their expressions a mixture of sadness and anger. They'd always known the world was changing, that humans were becoming more numerous and daring in their explorations. But they had always believed their cave to be safe, hidden from prying eyes by layers of stone and secrecy.

Paka knelt beside the disturbed earth, his hand brushing against a patch of soil as if willing it to return to its undisturbed state. "What if we hide the entrance again, mother?" he asked hopefully. "Maybe they won't come back."

Omaki shook her head. "If they've been here once, they may come again. We can't risk it. Even if we stay and hide the entrance, they might return—and next time, they might bring more of their kind." There was a resigned silence among them, the weight of Omaki's words settling heavily on each one of them. For generations, their cave had been a place of safety, a place where they could live in peace and solitude. Now, that peace had been shattered by strangers, and the reality of their vulnerability pressed upon them with painful clarity.

Asha clenched her fists, her voice bitter. "They don't care about the land like we do. They stomp through it, leave it ruined and damaged." Her anger radiated through the group, a shared resentment for the way humans moved through the world without thought. Omaki, a calming presence amidst the rising tension said, "I know, Asha, but we must think of the clan. Anger will only make this harder."

Raela spoke up, her voice trembling. "Where will we go? The cave has been our home for so long. There's nowhere else like it." Omaki took a deep breath, the full weight of leadership upon her. She'd spent her life in these caves, raising her family here, she and Taron guiding the clan through hardships. Leaving felt unnatural, painful, but she knew it was their only option. The safety of her clan came before all else.

"We'll find a new home," she said. "We'll travel together and seek out a place as safe as this one was."

The group nodded, absorbing the reality of her words. Leaving would not be easy, and the journey ahead would be filled with uncertainty. But as they stood there, looking upon the disturbed ground and the remnants of human presence, they knew that staying was no longer an option.

With one last, lingering look at their cave, Omaki turned away, leading her them into the unknown, a sense of both loss and resilience flowing through the group. The journey ahead would be long, but together, they would find a way forward.

39

MEMORIES

As the clan settled into silence after Omaki's announcement, Adanowa sat apart, his eyes trained on the ground, his mind miles away. The revelation that humans had found their cave struck him deeper than it did any other member of the clan. The sight of their footprints, the broken branches, and the evidence of intrusion were all too familiar. He had seen it before, years ago. And he had lost everything because of it.

Kabota noticed Adanowa's distant expression, concern in his voice. "Adanowa, you're quiet. I can only imagine what this means to you."

Adanowa barely reacted, his mind drifting through a haze of memories. In his mind, he was back on that Appalachian mountain ridge, the sights and smells filling his senses, the first sharp awareness that he was being watched creeping over him. It had been a day that changed his life forever, a day that marked the beginning of the end.

The sun shone brightly that day, filtering through the thick canopy of trees lining the Appalachian mountains, casting dappled shadows on the winding path. Adanowa was only a youngster then, though his senses were sharp and attuned to the land. His family had taught him well, instilling in him the caution needed to avoid human interaction. His father, Nado, and mother, Kila, had emphasized time and again: the humans were dangerous, untrustworthy, and they protected their territories with a force they didn't hesitate to use.

But curiosity was a powerful thing, and Adanowa had grown up hearing distant tales of humans and the strange places they created. He was careful, following the narrow deer trails and avoiding the main path. But his curiosity betrayed him. That day, he had lingered too long near the trail, catching a glimpse of two hikers—a man and a woman with bright, unfamiliar gear and voices that carried through the trees. He hadn't meant for them to see him; he had been perfectly still, his form blending with the shadows.

But as luck would have it, the woman's eyes had swept the ridge, and she had spotted him, her voice filled with alarm and awe as she pointed him out to her companion.

"Look! Did you see that?" she had gasped, her voice louder than the forest allowed.

He had run then, darting back into the forest. He'd hoped they would forget what they'd seen, that they would dismiss it as nothing more than a trick of the light. But he was wrong. Within hours, his family had sensed the disturbance, a new and foreign energy in their territory. Helicopters and military vehicles had arrived, a wall of machines and men encroaching on their sanctuary. Forest rangers had been the first wave, scouring the area for traces of the strange sighting, but when they found evidence—a footprint, a hint of their presence—they reported it up the chain.

The military, on high alert for anything unexplainable, had responded with overwhelming force.

The next few days were a nightmare, one that still haunted Adanowa's dreams. The forest, usually a place of peace and shelter, became a war zone. His family had no choice but to hide, but the humans came with strange devices and relentless drive, their determination unfaltering. One night, they cornered his family in a narrow valley, too close to human roads and civilization. His father and mother had urged him to run, to use his small size and speed to escape. Adanowa had resisted, but his father's stern gaze left no room for argument.

"This is not your fight," Nado had said, his voice filled with a calm strength. "Your path is different. Go now, Adanowa, and don't look back."

But looking back was all he could do. He had hidden among the thick ferns, watching as his parents faced the line of humans, their hands raised in a desperate attempt to show they were no threat. But the humans had not understood; they didn't want to understand. Orders were barked, guns raised, and the forest was filled with the deafening crack of gunfire.

Adanowa's world shattered as he watched his parents fall, their bodies crumpling to the earth, their eyes open in a final, shocked silence. The soldiers advanced, checking for signs of life, but found only death and empty resistance. Adanowa was paralyzed, as he willed himself to stay hidden. He wanted to scream, to run out and confront them, but his father's last words echoed in his mind, a reminder that only survival mattered.

Hours later, the noise of heavy machinery filled the forest as helicopters hovered over the scene. He watched, numb and unseeing, as they loaded his parents' bodies into the helicopters, lifting them away as if they were nothing more than specimens. The blades of the helicopter sent the forest into a whirlwind, the gust scattering leaves and branches as Adanowa lay beneath the ferns, waiting for the nightmare to end.

The memory faded, and Adanowa found himself back in the clearing, fists tight at his sides, his jaw set. The pain of that day burned within, as fresh as all those years ago. The humans had taken everything from him—his family, his childhood, his trust. And now, even here, even among his new clan, they had intruded once more, violating the one place he had come to consider safe.

The urge to seek revenge stirred within him, filling him with a dark, familiar rage that he had spent years trying to bury. It had taken him a long time to find peace after his parents' deaths, to believe in the possibility of building a life without hatred. His new clan had given him purpose, grounding him in their traditions and bonds.

But now that peace felt fragile, like a thin layer of ice over deep, raging waters.

Kabota, sensing the storm brewing within him, approached cautiously. "Adanowa, I know this is hard. None of us can truly understand what this means for you." Adanowa met his gaze, his voice low and filled with a barely restrained anger. "You don't know what they've taken from me, Kabota. And now, they come here. They've taken enough."

Kabota placed a calming hand on his shoulder, grounding him. "I know you've been through more than any of us, but this clan—you belong here now. We're your family. We'll find a way through this together." Adanowa nodded, but the hatred inside him smoldered, a fire waiting for the right spark to ignite.

That night, Adanowa lay awake, thoughts racing through his mind, each one feeding his anger. He could still hear the sound of helicopters, see the figures of the soldiers as they took his parents away. His heart pounded with the old pain, but now, it was paired with something new—a sense of purpose, a need for action.

His clan had found a new family in him, had shown him kindness and compassion. But the humans—the humans knew no compassion. They had taken his family once, and now they threatened to do it again.

The thought of hunting them down himself began to take shape, a desire to confront them as his parents had not been able to do. He imagined himself in the forest, tracking the humans, ambushing them in the places they least expected, striking them with the precision and ruthlessness they had shown his family.

But then he saw his new family—the faces of Kabota, Asha, Omaki, and the young ones—and doubt crept in. Was revenge worth risking everything he had built? Was it worth becoming the very thing he despised?

He took a deep breath, his mind a tangle of emotions. The choice lay before him: he could either plunge back into the darkness of his hatred and seek vengeance, or he could stay, using his strength to protect those he had come to care for. The decision weighed heavily, a choice that could either destroy him or save him.

As dawn broke, Adanowa rose, his resolve unsteady but present. He would face the humans, but not alone. He would bring his clan into his plan, sharing his story with them, making them understand the stakes. Together, they could find a way to protect their future, without letting hatred consume them.

But if the humans came too close again, Adanowa would not hold back.

40

BURDEN

Omaki stood at the edge of the forest, watching the morning mist settle across the valley. Her heart weighed heavy with the knowledge she carried—knowledge that could mean life or death for her sons and her clan. Her gaze drifted northward, toward where Erek and Varo had chosen to stay after the Great Hunt, embracing new lives with the Stone Ridge and Riverbend clans. She respected their choices but had never anticipated such a separation would be marred by this danger.

With the sighting of Koda by a drone and the likelihood that the humans had reported their discovery to higher authorities, the clan's sanctuary was no longer safe. Even now, they were preparing to leave, gathering their few belongings and saying quiet farewells to the cave that had protected them for generations. The thought of her sons being caught unaware, vulnerable and unprotected, sent a shiver through her. She could not leave them in the dark.

Taking a steadying breath, Omaki cupped her hands around her mouth, sending a call through the trees—a unique whistle that only her sons would recognize. She waited, her heartbeat quickening as she listened for a response. Moments passed in tense silence before a familiar echo returned, faint but clear. Relief washed over her, knowing her call had reached them. Soon, she would have the chance to warn them, to ensure they understood the gravity of the threat facing their people.

Back at the cave, the atmosphere was somber, each member moving with quiet efficiency but heavy hearts. The cave had been their home, a place of safety and memories, and leaving it behind felt like abandoning a piece of their souls. However, the discovery of Koda by the drone had altered everything. They all knew what was at stake.

Koda stood to one side, his guilt his only thought as he watched the others pack. Meika, approached him.

"It wasn't your fault, Koda," she said gently, though worry thickened her own voice. "None of us could have predicted this." Koda gave a tight nod, his gaze distant. "I just can't help but feel that I've put us all in danger. If I hadn't been out there..."

"There's no time for blame," Omaki interjected, her voice strong as she joined them. "We move forward now. It's the only choice we have."

As the clan continued their preparations, Adanowa remained at the edge of the group, his expression tense. The news of the humans' discovery had shaken him to the core, stirring memories he had long tried to bury. He glanced around at the others, at their expressions of uncertainty, and felt a surge of anger mingled with fear. He knew all too well what the humans were capable of, and the possibility of the military finding them sent chills through his blood.

He finally spoke with a quiet intensity that caught the attention of those around him. "The humans won't stop until they have what they want. If they come with their machines and soldiers with guns... they will show no mercy. I've seen it before." The clan members looked at him with concern and respect. They knew bits and pieces of Adanowa's past, that he had lost his family to the very threat they now faced, but few understood the full extent of his trauma. Adanowa's warning adding a new urgency to their movements.

Omaki met his gaze with understanding. "We will be careful,

Adanowa. But we cannot let fear drive us into hiding. We will find a new home—a place the humans will never touch."

Her words, though strong, could not entirely dispel the unease that clung to the group. They were leaving behind everything they knew, heading into the unknown with only the hope of safety to guide them. The weight of the moment pressed down upon them, but they continued, each step bringing them closer to the path that would lead them to find a new home.

Several hours later, after winding through dense forest and steep inclines, the clan finally reached the place they had arranged to meet Erek and Varo. The area was quiet, the sunlight filtering softly through the trees, casting dappled shadows across the forest floor. Omaki's heart ached as she spotted her sons, their faces lighting up with joy at the sight of their clan. But the happiness faded quickly as they saw the tension etched on each face, the strain that hinted at something far more troubling.

"Mother," Erek said, his voice filled with a mixture of relief and worry as he approached her. "What happened? Why are you all here?"

Omaki embraced him, the strength of her love for her sons pushing aside her worry for just a moment. She pulled back, looking from Erek to Varo, her expression serious.

"We've come to warn you," she began, her tone grave. "The humans have found our cave. We're leaving."

The shock on Erek and Varo's faces was immediate, a flash of disbelief quickly replaced by anger and concern.

"What? How?" Varo asked, his fists clenching. "How could they have found it?"

"Koda was spotted," Omaki explained. "By a drone. We're almost certain the sighting was reported to the forest service, and if they escalate this... we could be looking at a military operation."

Erek's face went pale. He had heard tales of human drones, machines that flew high above the forest, watching and recording everything below. "So, they know we exist."

Omaki nodded, her gaze steady. "Yes. And it's only a matter of time before they come looking."

The group stood in silence, absorbing the weight of her words. Adanowa stepped forward, his jaw set as he looked at Erek and Varo. "This isn't just about discovery. If the military gets involved, they won't stop until they find every last one of us. I've seen it happen before—they hunt without mercy, without hesitation."

Erek and Varo exchanged a troubled glance, their new lives suddenly clouded by the past they had tried to distance themselves from. The allure of Stone Ridge and Riverbend, the dreams they had begun to build, now seemed fragile and vulnerable under the shadow of this new threat.

The silence that followed Omaki's words was thick and uneasy. Each member of the clan felt the weight of what lay ahead, the memories of their once-safe cave now shadowed by the very real threat of discovery.

"Koda was seen?" Erek's voice was filled with disbelief. "After all these years... how could we be so unlucky?"

Koda, who stood nearby, shifted uncomfortably, his guilt evident as he looked down. "I didn't know they were watching from above. I thought I was alone. We've always been safe in the high forested areas before," he said, his voice a mix of sorrow and frustration.

"You can't blame yourself," Omaki said gently. "This was bound to happen one day. It's not your fault. The humans are growing more curious and invasive. What matters now is that we protect ourselves and stay hidden."

Varo looked from Koda to his mother, his concern deepening. "But if the humans send more than just drones—if they send people, with all their equipment and their knowledge of tracking—they won't stop at finding the cave. They'll come looking for all of us."

Adanowa, who had been listening quietly, took a sharp breath and stepped forward, his gaze hard and unyielding. His presence, normally calm and controlled, radiated a simmering tension that none could ignore.

"They won't just 'look' for us," he said, his voice low and laced with a dark certainty. "If the military gets involved, they'll hunt us down like animals. And they won't stop until they've destroyed everything in their path." The weight of his words struck the group with a chilling finality, each clan member turning to face him, their expressions filled with a mixture of fear and curiosity. Though they all knew Adanowa's story, few had ever heard him speak of it directly.

Erek met Adanowa's gaze, sensing the intensity in his eyes. "You've... seen this before, haven't you?"

Adanowa's jaw tightened, his gaze distant as memories surfaced, sharp and painful. "Yes. I've seen it before. And it's a memory that has haunted me every day of my life." He took a deep breath, steadying himself before continuing. "Years ago, my family and I thought we were safe, too. We lived in the highlands, well-hidden from human eyes, or so we thought. But one day, just like Koda, I was seen. A group of hikers spotted me along the Appalachian trail."

He paused, the memory raw in his voice. "What happened afterward was a nightmare. The humans sent out search parties, forest rangers, then, when they saw what they were dealing with, they sent in the military. They came with helicopters, machines, weapons meant to end lives, not protect them."

The clan listened in rapt silence, the fear in their faces deepening as Adanowa continued.

"I was just a young one then, but I watched from the shadows as they hunted us down, my family and me. My parents tried to reason with them, tried to show them we weren't a threat. But the humans didn't care—they only saw something they couldn't understand, something they couldn't control. And so they killed them. Both my parents, gone within seconds, their bodies taken away like trophies."

A hush settled over the group, each member struggling to absorb the horror Adanowa had lived through. For many, this was the first time they truly understood why he carried such a deep, seething distrust of humans. His fears were not born from simple prejudice or misunderstanding; they were the scars of unimaginable loss.

Adanowa's gaze sharpened, turning back to Erek and Varo. "If they're coming again, they won't stop until they find us all. The military doesn't leave room for questions—they will kill us if they see us as a threat. We cannot be careless. We cannot hope they'll simply go away."

Varo, his face pale, looked down at the ground, processing Adanowa's words. Erek, too, felt the weight of the decision. While he had chosen to stay with the Stone Ridge clan, to pursue a new life with Kora, the idea of abandoning his family in their time of need felt like a betrayal.

"So what do we do?" Varo finally asked. "Do we keep running forever? Keep hiding until they finally give up?"

Omaki looked at her sons. "That may be our only option," she replied quietly. "If they see us, they won't care that we're no threat. They'll see us as nothing more than something strange and dangerous. Adanowa is right. We can't risk being seen again."

She took a deep breath, steeling herself as she addressed Erek and Varo. "Which is why I need both of you to return to the Stone Ridge and Riverbend clans."

Erek's eyes widened in protest. "But, Mother—"

"No," Omaki interrupted. "You've chosen a new life with Kora and Rina, and that is where you belong now. Your safety lies with them, away from this threat. We can't risk you being here with us if the humans decide to send more search teams. Your lives matter to me more than anything, and I won't let you throw them away."

The plea in her voice was unmistakable, a mother's fierce love battling with the knowledge that she couldn't protect her children forever. Erek's throat tightened as he looked at her, torn between his loyalty to his family and the new connections he had begun to forge. Varo, too, felt the tug of loyalty and duty to his mother and clan, yet he couldn't ignore the bond he was forming with Kora.

"But what if we can help?" Erek asked, his voice breaking slightly. "What if we can do something—anything—to keep you safe?"

Omaki shook her head, her expression firm. "You've already helped more than enough by warning us, by giving us the support we needed in the past. But this—this is different. If you stay, you'll only put yourselves in more danger. And if something were to happen to either of you..." She trailed off, the horror of losing her sons too painful to express.

Adanowa stepped forward, his expression softening as he looked at Erek and Varo. "Your mother is right. The risk is too great, not just for you, but for everyone. If we're to survive this, we need to be as invisible as the forest itself. Your presence only makes us more visible."

Varo exhaled slowly, the truth of their words settling heavily in his heart. He looked at Erek, seeing his own conflict mirrored in his brother's eyes. The pull of family, of loyalty and love, was undeniable, but so was the promise they had made to Kora and Rina, to stay and build a life together.

Finally, Erek nodded. "I'll go," he said. "I'll go back to Stone Ridge, and I'll keep my distance. But if you need us—if you need help —I'll be there in a heartbeat. I swear it."

Varo nodded in agreement. "The same goes for me. We'll be close enough to protect you if it comes to that." Omaki smiled, her expression a mixture of sadness and pride as she looked at her sons. "Thank you, both of you. I know this isn't easy, but it's what's best for you— and for us. I will send word as soon as we find a new home, a place where we can all be safe."

Erek embraced her, his arms wrapping tightly around his mother, the realization of their separation sinking in. "Promise me you'll be careful," he said. "Promise me you won't take any unnecessary risks." Omaki nodded, as tears flowed down her cheeks. "I promise, my son."

Adanowa looked on. He understood the pain of separation, the unspoken fear of what lay ahead, but he also saw the strength in each of them, a strength forged in survival and bound by love. As the first hints of dusk settled over the forest, Erek and Varo stepped back, taking one last look at their family and the life they were leaving behind. The decision to walk away felt like a wound, raw and unhealed, but it was a sacrifice they made willingly for the safety of those they loved.

Omaki raised her hand in farewell, a silent promise passing between them. She would keep them safe, no matter the cost, and they would honor that by building the future they had chosen. With one last glance, Erek and Varo turned and began their journey back, their hearts heavy but resolved.

The clan watched them go, the weight of their departure settling over them. Omaki held back her tears, knowing she had done what was necessary, even if it tore at her heart. She turned to Adanowa, a shared understanding passing between them.

"We will survive this," she said, her voice steady but fierce. "We have to."

Adanowa nodded. "And if the humans come for us, they will regret it."

Together, they turned back toward the forest. They would protect their people, their way of life, and each other, no matter what threats lay in the shadows. The journey to their new home had begun.

41

RELOCATION

The morning was quiet as each member of the clan braced for the journey into higher elevations. Omaki moved among them, offering quiet encouragement, her presence a source of strength for those feeling the uncertainty of leaving the familiar valley. As the group prepared, she glanced back one final time at the valley, committing its memory to heart before she led her family away.

The path upward was steep and challenging, a mixture of rocky terrain and thick undergrowth that tested the endurance of the younger members and required the support of the elders. Asha, moved to the front of the line, choosing their route with precision, ensuring they stayed hidden and away from any known human paths. The air grew cooler as they ascended, the valley below fading from view as they left behind their once-safe haven.

Koda, walking beside Meika, glanced up at the towering cliffs ahead. "Do you think we'll find a place as secure as the cave?"

Meika shrugged. "If mother has faith that we'll find safety, then so do I."

Adanowa, overhearing their conversation, moved up beside them. His expression was distant, yet resolved, as he scanned their surroundings with a cautious eye. "We must remain vigilant," he said.

"The higher we climb, the closer we come to safety. But until then, we can't let our guard down." They pressed on, the sun rising higher in the sky as they moved through a dense thicket that gave way to a sweeping view of the surrounding mountains. From here, the landscape was rugged and untouched, a vast expanse of green and stone that promised isolation. But the higher they climbed, the more they felt the fatigue of the journey, each step a reminder of the safety they'd left behind.

Omaki back in the lead set a steady pace, her gaze fixed on the horizon as she led her clan forward. Though her heart ached from the separation from Erek and Varo, she felt a deep conviction that their sacrifice was necessary for the safety of the clan. She had to trust that they would find strength in their new lives, just as she sought to find strength for the rest of the clan in this uncertain journey.

After two days of arduous travel, the clan paused on a narrow plateau, the air crisp and thin. Asha, who had scouted ahead, returned to the group, her eyes alight with excitement. "I've found something," she said, her voice barely containing her awe. "A cave, hidden between three cliffs. It's unlike anything we've ever seen—a natural fortress, almost impossible to see unless you know where to look."

The clan exchanged hopeful glances, and Omaki nodded for Asha to lead the way. They followed her through a dense grove, emerging on the other side to find themselves standing before an awe-inspiring sight. Towering cliffs loomed around them, their jagged edges casting shadows over a massive cave entrance, partially obscured by thick vines and a grove of towering pines. The cave itself seemed to open like the mouth of a giant, dark and welcoming, while the cliffs provided a natural shield on three sides, creating a sense of security unlike any they had known.

Omaki's heart swelled with hope as she took in the scene. The area surrounding the cave was lush, with thick forests teeming with life. A river, broad and fast-flowing, wound through the landscape nearby, its banks lined with berry bushes and wild fruit trees. It was as if the land itself had opened up to provide for them, offering both sustenance and protection.

"This place..." Meika said, her voice filled with awe. "It feels... sacred."

Adanowa stepped forward, his expression thoughtful as he examined their surroundings. "This place will protect us well," he said, his voice filled with cautious optimism. "But we must still be careful. Humans are clever, and if they've reached us once, they can do it again." Omaki nodded, but relief settled over her. This cave, shielded and surrounded by natural resources, felt like a gift—an answer to their prayers for safety.

As the clan settled into their new sanctuary, Erek and Varo were making their way back to the Stone Ridge and Riverbend clans, each weighed by the recent parting and the pressing responsibility to share the dangers with their people. Erek's heart ached as he remembered his mother's words, her insistence that he and Varo return to their new lives, safe from the looming threat. But even as he carried her wishes, he felt the unease of their vulnerability.

They parted ways at a familiar ridge, Varo heading toward Stone Ridge territory while Erek moved through the forest, his steps guiding him back to the Riverbend clan. As he approached the cluster of shelters nestled among the trees, he spotted Rina, her face breaking into a smile as she saw him.

"Erek!" she called, moving to embrace him, her arms warm and welcoming. But her expression shifted as she sensed the weight in his gaze. "What happened?"

Erek took her hand, leading her to a quiet spot where they could talk. "The humans found our cave," he said quietly. "We had to leave. The clan is heading to higher ground, but the risk is... greater than we thought."

Rina's eyes widened, her hand tightening around his. "Erek, are they safe?"

"They're safe for now," he replied, his voice steady but laced with worry. "But this isn't over. The humans are relentless, and if they find us again... we could all be in danger."

Rina nodded, her face resolute. "Then we must let everyone know. If the Riverbend and Stone Ridge clans are at risk, they deserve to be prepared."

Meanwhile, Varo had reached the heart of Stone Ridge territory, where Kora awaited him. The joy in her eyes at his return quickly faded as he explained the recent events. "If the humans found your family's cave, then we're all at risk," she said quietly, taking his hand. "We've always been cautious, but this changes things. We need to discuss this with the others."

With the support of Kora and Rina, Erek and Varo arranged meetings with their respective clans, urging caution and explaining the potential danger posed by the humans. In Stone Ridge, the elders listened intently as Varo recounted the warning, the severity of his tone casting a solemn mood over the group.

"We don't know how long the humans have been watching, or how many of them are aware of us," Varo said. "But we do know that if they find us, they won't simply walk away."

One of the elders, nodded thoughtfully. "We've lived in these woods for generations, but the humans have grown bolder. We need to be vigilant, to ensure they never see more than what they're meant to."

In riverbend, erek shared similar concerns with the leaders, stressing the need for stealth and secrecy. The clan responded with both worry and determination, each member resolving to protect their home, even if it meant moving farther into the wild. Rina placed a hand on erek's shoulder as the meeting concluded, her gaze steady. "we'll stay safe, erek. But knowing the danger is out there will make us stronger, more aware."

42

ASSESSMENT

The morning sun cast soft light over the clearing outside the new cave, its rays filtering through the pines and illuminating the rocky walls that sheltered the clan. As they moved about, assessing the area, cautious relief permeated the group. Each member of the clan recognized the unique protection the cliffs offered, their natural walls making it difficult for intruders to stumble upon them. It felt, for the first time in days, like a place where they could breathe a little easier.

Omaki surveyed the cave entrance, eyes narrowing in concentration as she mentally mapped the safest arrangement for the clan's essential spaces. The main living area would be situated deeper within, where the light was dim but ample for privacy and warmth. Gathering spots for shared meals and discussions would be kept closer to the front. Meanwhile, they would take turns as lookouts near the edges of their new territory, serving as the first line of defense against any intruders.

"Meika, can you organize a team to clear the entrance and set up wind barriers?" Omaki called, her voice carrying with quiet authority. "The air is sharp here; we'll need those barriers to keep the warmth inside the cave."

Meika nodded, rallying the younger clan members to help with the task. They began gathering stones and fallen branches to construct low walls and natural partitions at the entrance, their arrangements strategic to break the wind while blending seamlessly into the surroundings. The clan moved carefully, keeping noise and visibility to a minimum as they worked.

Meanwhile, Asha, Kabota, and Koda set up a lookout system. They climbed the cliffs that bordered the cave, choosing high, natural perches with unobstructed views of the valley below. Any approach by humans or other potential threats would be visible from these positions. Koda, weighted by his recent drone encounter, worked with a solemn diligence that did not go unnoticed.

"Are you all right, Koda?" Asha asked as they secured their positions with natural footholds and vines, ensuring they could climb back down easily and without leaving traces.

Koda paused, his gaze lingering on the forest stretching endlessly below. "I keep thinking about what happened back there. I should have been more careful."

"Son, we all make mistakes. What matters is that you're here now, helping keep the clan safe. We're stronger for it."

Koda managed a small nod, his expression softening with gratitude. Together, they continued their work, setting up a silent alert system using carefully arranged stones and leaves that would rustle or clatter with the slightest disturbance, allowing them to signal the clan quickly if anything approached.

As the clan settled in, routines anchored them to their new surroundings. Meika and Raela took on mapping the area, cataloging edible plants, herbs, and small game trails. The abundance of resources reassured them about surviving winter, yet being close to human paths meant they gathered quietly and efficiently, never straying far from the cliffs.

Paka organized regular forages for berries, nuts, and medicinal herbs. He learned how to conceal his tracks, to leave no signs of their presence. Every move was calculated, every action taken with the understanding that discovery would mean an end to their sanctuary.

One afternoon, as Paka and Meika made their way deeper into the forest to collect wild onions, Meika noticed a small footprint left by one of the clan. She quickly erased it with a sweep of her hand, her gaze serious as she addressed the group once they returned to the cave.

"We leave no trace," she reminded them, her voice steady. "Every footprint, every broken branch could be a message to those who wish to harm us. We move like shadows in the forest."

Everyone nodded solemnly. The younger generation was learning quickly, adapting to the realities of their new life with a resilience that reassured the elders.

The long, quiet evenings inside the cave brought closeness the clan hadn't experienced in some time. Gathered around low-burning fires, they shared stories and laughter. The presence of the cliffs and the secluded river nearby gave them a degree of comfort, yet they knew that their vigilance could never waver.

Adanowa sat apart from the main group one evening, his gaze fixed on the cave's entrance as though expecting something to approach from the darkness beyond. His mind wandered to the memories of his family's last days, haunted by the feeling of vulnerability he had carried ever since. But as he looked around at the clan members who now surrounded him, he felt a deep sense of responsibility and purpose. This was his family now, and he would do whatever it took to keep them safe.

Omaki, noticing his quiet isolation, approached him, lowering herself to sit beside him. "You look troubled, Adanowa," she said, her voice soft yet filled with concern.

He hesitated, then nodded. "Sometimes, I think we're fooling ourselves. The humans... They don't stop. They don't forget." He looked at her, his gaze intense. "But this time, I won't let them take anyone from me. Not again."

"You've been through more than any of us, Adanowa. And your strength keeps us safe. But we must remember why we're here— because we want to live, not just survive. Our vigilance will keep us hidden, but our connections, our shared purpose... That's what will keep us alive."

Adanowa looked down, her words sinking in. He knew she was right, that his fears, while valid, should not rob him of the peace they all deserved to find. He nodded, a small gesture of acceptance, allowing himself to believe this new place might indeed be a sanctuary.

43

NORMALCY

With each passing day, the clan's routines solidified, and a sense of normalcy began to return. Yet, reminders of their need for caution were woven into each task, each movement outside the protection of the cave. Asha and Kabota continued their lookout shifts, rotating with the others to ensure that someone was always watching, ready to alert the clan at the first sign of danger.

During a quiet moment on one of his shifts, Kabota watched a hawk circle above, its shadow gliding across the valley below. He marveled at how it remained invisible until the moment it swooped down, striking its prey with precision and silence. The bird became a symbol for him, a reminder that to survive, the clan needed to become as elusive as the hawk, hidden until the moment they chose to be seen.

As he kept his eyes on the horizon, he whispered to himself, "We will stay hidden, like you. We will remain out of reach."

In the evenings, Omaki continued to gather the clan around, sharing stories and reinforcing the importance of their bond. Each tale she told reminded them of their resilience, of their ability to thrive no matter the odds. She spoke of ancestors who had traversed great distances to find safety, who had survived wars and natural disasters, all with the same resolve that now guided them.

"We are stronger than we know," she would say, her eyes shining with quiet pride. "As long as we stand together, we are unstoppable."

These gatherings strengthened the clan's resolve, solidifying the understanding that each of them played a crucial role in their survival. It was not just about hiding or escaping discovery—it was about creating a life filled with meaning, where every moment mattered.

Meanwhile, back with the Stone Ridge and Riverbend clans, Erek and Varo carried the memory of their farewell with them as they resumed their lives. They could feel the distance from their family as a physical ache, yet their decision to stay with Kora and Rina was forti-fied by the knowledge that they were helping to protect their clan in a different way. Each day, they shared the stories of their own clan's struggles with their new families, urging them to remain cautious and respectful of the boundaries between their lives and the human world.

One evening, as they sat around with Kora and Rina, Erek shared a memory of his last night in the cave. "There's something about the way we lived back then that I'll always carry with me—the unity, the understanding that each of us mattered. Here, it's different, but that connection is something I hope we'll build, too."

Rina took his hand. "We'll create that unity, Erek, but we'll do it here, together. And with every step forward, we honor what you've left behind."

Kora placed her hand over Varo's, her gaze filled with quiet deter-mination. "Your journey is our journey now. We'll protect this life we're building together and keep each other safe."

As the night deepened, Erek and Varo felt at peace knowing they could honor their past while embracing their new lives. Though the separation from their clan weighed on them, they knew their vigi-lance and love would continue to guide them all.

The dawn light was muted, soft shadows spilling over the rugged terrain as Erek and Rina made their way through a dense grove of trees. The air was crisp and filled with the familiar scents of pine and earth, but there was something else beneath it—a faint, acrid smell that lingered in the air. Smoke.

Erek paused, his senses sharpening as he scanned the horizon. The subtle aroma of burning wood mixed with the crisp morning air, an unnatural presence in the forest. His pulse quickened, and he glanced at Rina, who had noticed it too, her gaze distant and alert.

"Do you smell it?" she whispered, her tone laced with concern.

Erek nodded, his jaw set. "Humans. They're nearby."

They continued onward in silence, ears tuned to the sounds around them, each step careful and measured. Soon, the faint hum of engines echoed through the forest, growing louder as they drew closer. The unnatural sound grated against the tranquility of the woods. This was not the first time they had heard humans encroaching upon their territory, but the persistence of the noise and the smoke suggested this was more than just passing hikers.

Later that morning, they met up with Varo and Kora, who had taken a different path to survey the surrounding area. Varo's expression was tense as he looked at Erek, confirming what they both feared.

"They're pushing farther in every day," Varo said, casting a wary glance at the distant ridges. "And it's not just one or two campers. I saw at least three separate fires smoldering in the valley."

Kora crossed her arms, her eyes flashing with anger and concern. "They're relentless. It's as if they know we're here, as if they're seeking us out."

The four of them exchanged a look, each feeling the weight of the unspoken threat. This wasn't an ordinary intrusion. The humans were persistent, methodical, and relentless in their pursuit. And the signs all pointed to one grim possibility: the humans were hunting something—or someone—specific.

"We should warn the clans," Rina said finally, her voice steady. "Everyone needs to know just how close they're getting."

Erek nodded, his expression hardening with resolve. "we need to prepare for whatever comes next. This isn't the time for us to be caught off guard."

44

SOLIDARITY

By midday, both the Stone Ridge and Riverbend clans had gathered in their respective council clearings, leaders and scouts discussing the increasingly urgent situation. Erek and Varo, along with Rina and Kora, presented their findings, detailing the presence of the humans, their fires, and the unmistakable sound of engines.

The Stone Ridge elders listened closely, their faces grim and contemplative. Mira, an elder known for her cautious nature, spoke first, her gaze steady as she addressed the group.

"This land has always been our home," Mira said, her voice laced with quiet defiance. "But we cannot ignore the signs. If the humans are actively seeking us, we must consider every option, including the possibility of relocating."

Kora stepped forward, her voice calm yet strong. "Relocation may not be enough. These humans aren't just wandering through— they're organized, equipped, and determined. We need to think defensively, to set up barriers and ways to evade them if they get too close."

At Riverbend, similar sentiments arose, though the tension was punctuated by a fierce resolve to defend their territory. One of the younger hunters, Raek, voiced a more aggressive opinion.

"We can't hide forever," Raek said, his tone heated. "If they're coming for us, then maybe it's time we show them we're not to be trifled with."

Rina placed a calming hand on his shoulder. "We mustn't underestimate their strength. The humans have weapons and technology we can't match. Attacking them directly would only bring more of them."

Varo backed her up, recounting the warnings his family had given him and Erek before their separation. "I know it's difficult, but we have to think of survival first. Our goal is to keep the clan safe, not to seek conflict. We'll prepare to defend ourselves if it comes to that, but we must avoid drawing attention."

The two clans ultimately reached a consensus to begin preparing defenses while remaining as hidden as possible. Their goal would be to evade detection, setting up strategies to mislead the humans and keep their sanctuaries concealed. But despite their unity, an undercurrent of fear and tension rippled through the clans as they braced for what seemed to be an inevitable clash.

Determined to understand the humans' tactics, Erek and Varo set out the next day with two other scouts, Jarek from Stone Ridge and Sylia from Riverbend. Their mission was to observe the encampments from a safe distance, gathering any information that might help the clans avoid detection.

The four moved in silence, blending into the shadows as they crept closer to the human camp. From their vantage point on a ridge overlooking the valley, they could see rows of tents and vehicles, some with insignia that suggested a formal organization. Equipment was laid out in meticulous order—maps, portable devices, and rows of strange instruments.

One man in particular, clad in tactical gear, gestured to a map, explaining something to the others. His movements were precise, his demeanor suggesting a seasoned leader. Around him, others listened intently, nodding as he gave instructions. This was no casual group of enthusiasts; these people were prepared, systematic, and well-organized.

"Look at their equipment," Varo whispered, his face grim. "They've got everything—tracking devices, communication tools, even drones."

Jarek shook his head in disbelief. "They're more prepared than I feared. If they're this organized, they won't stop until they've found what they're looking for."

Erek's gaze hardened as he watched the humans, his mind racing. They had to act quickly. Every day that passed meant the humans were one step closer to discovering their people, one step closer to shattering the peace they had tried so hard to preserve.

"We need to report this back to the clans," Erek said. "They need to understand just how serious this is."

With a final, wary glance at the encampment below, the scouts turned and retreated into the forest, their movements silent and swift as they returned to deliver their grim findings.

Upon hearing the scouts' report, the Stone Ridge and Riverbend clans wasted no time in strengthening their defenses. Leaders from both clans worked together to set up escape routes through the densest parts of the forest, pathways concealed by natural foliage that would allow them to retreat quickly if needed.

Kora and Rina, alongside other skilled gatherers, took charge of preparing supplies for an emergency. They stored herbs, dried foods, and other essentials in hidden caches throughout the forest, each one marked subtly so that only the clans would know their locations. Their preparations were quiet yet thorough, each cache carefully concealed to avoid detection.

Varo and Erek, meanwhile, coordinated with the scouts to establish communication systems—signals made from bird calls or patterns of stones that would alert clan members if the humans drew too close. The signals were simple but effective, and they hoped they would allow them to stay one step ahead.

During one of these preparations, Kora glanced at Varo, her eyes filled with determination. "We've faced hardships before, but this... This feels different."

Varo nodded, his jaw set with resolve. "It is different. But we have each other, and that's something the humans can't take from us. As long as we're united, we'll endure."

Rina, overhearing their conversation, placed a hand on Erek's shoulder. "This won't break us. If anything, it's only made us stronger."

Erek looked at her, his face softening despite the tension. "Then we hold fast, no matter what comes. We won't give them what they want."

Days passed, and the clans adapted to their new routines, every member vigilant and prepared for whatever might come. Yet the signs of the humans' presence grew more constant, the roar of ATVs echoing through the valleys, the scent of smoke lingering on the breeze. Each night, the clans waited in tense anticipation, braced for the moment when the humans would draw close enough to confront.

45

CURIOSITY

Late one evening, as the sounds of engines grew loud in the distance, Erek and Varo climbed to one of the lookout points on a nearby ridge. From there, they saw a faint glow on the horizon, the humans' fires burning through the night. The sight filled them with grim determination, a reminder of the sacrifices they had made to protect their families and the lives they had chosen to build.

Kora joined them, her face drawn but resolute. She placed a hand on Varo's arm, her voice steady. "No matter what happens, we'll face it together."

Rina, standing beside Erek, added softly, "We're stronger than they realize. And we're more connected to this land than they'll ever be."

The four stood in silence, eyes fixed on the distant fires, their hearts filled with shared determination. They would protect their people, their home, and each other, no matter the cost.

In the depths of the forest, the clans waited, united and unyielding, prepared to defend their sanctuary against the encroaching threat. The tension in the air was thick, with the promise that, if forced, they would fight for the lives they had built, even in the face of an unstoppable force.

The forest was still under the light of a waning moon, shadows stretching across the ground, as two juveniles of the Riverbend clan, Kaelen and Darek, crept along the tree line near a human campsite. The scent of smoke and cooked food wafted through the air, unfamiliar yet oddly enticing, drawing them in despite the stern warnings from their elders.

Kaelen crouched low, his eyes gleaming with excitement as he observed the humans gathered around their fire, their faces illuminated by the flickering flames. Darek shifted beside him, barely able to contain his eagerness.

"They're just sitting there, completely unaware," Darek whispered.

"Let's make them remember tonight," Kaelen replied with a mischievous grin, and without hesitation, he broke a few low branches, placing them deliberately near the trail that led away from the campsite. The snapping sounds echoed through the stillness, catching the attention of one of the men.

Encouraged by the reaction, Kaelen threw a small stone that landed near the edge of the campfire, earning a startled exclamation from one of the humans. Darek chuckled quietly, his confidence growing as he made low howling sounds followed by quick, rhythmic mouth pops. The humans sat up, heads darting around as they searched for the source of the sounds.

But just as the juveniles were preparing to slip away, the humans pulled out flashlights—high-powered beams that sliced through the dark, illuminating the tree line with a brightness that made Kaelen and Darek freeze. These were not ordinary flashlights; the light was far more powerful than anything they had seen before. The beams swept over them, and for a heartbeat, Kaelen and Darek found themselves exposed, their forms briefly visible in the light.

The realization hit them like a thunderclap: the humans could see them.

"Run!" Kaelen hissed, his voice taut with panic as he shoved Darek toward the shadows. The two juveniles sprinted away, their hearts pounding as they ducked and weaved through the trees, the distant sound of shouting and more lights chasing them until they were finally enveloped by the forest's darkness.

By morning, word of the juveniles' encounter had spread through the Riverbend clan, igniting a wave of fear and frustration. The elders were furious, scolding Kaelen and Darek for their recklessness, while others in the clan whispered anxiously about the humans' increasing vigilance. What had started as a harmless prank had now escalated into a potential threat to their survival.

One of the Riverbend leaders, Kalenna, gathered the members for an emergency meeting, her expression severe as she addressed the group.

"The humans are closer than we realized," she began, her tone grim. "And Kaelen and Darek's actions may have put us all at risk. We cannot afford to be careless—not when the safety of our entire clan is at stake."

Kaelen, still feeling the sting of embarrassment, looked down, ashamed. Darek, though remorseful, felt the injustice of the blame weighing on him. "We were just having fun," he said, though his voice held little conviction.

"There is no room for fun when our safety is in question," Kalenna replied sharply. "The humans now have proof of our presence, and they won't stop until they find more evidence. This may bring a wave of new dangers—not just for us, but for all clans nearby."

Her words hung in the air, sobering the group as they absorbed the weight of the situation. The decision was clear: they would need to reinforce their vigilance, to watch for signs of human activity and be prepared to leave if necessary.

46

COUNCIL

The following day, leaders from Stone Ridge, Riverbend, and a neighboring clan, Mistwood, gathered for a council meeting. The clans had shared the forest in peace for generations, bound by mutual respect and an unspoken alliance to protect one another from external threats. But the recent human activity had introduced a new strain, forcing them to confront the threat that could affect them all.

Erek and Varo attended on behalf of their clan, their faces etched with worry as they relayed the details of the juveniles' encounter. Rina and Kora stood by their sides, lending their support as the leaders listened intently.

"Kaelen and Darek's actions were reckless," Mira, an elder from Stone Ridge, said sternly, her eyes fixed on the Riverbend leader. "But we cannot let their mistake define our response. We must remain united in our approach."

A voice from the Mistwood clan, Larek's, interjected, his tone bristling with anger. "United? The humans are advancing with each passing day, and their persistence grows stronger. How do we know that hiding will keep us safe forever?"

"We don't," Rina replied, her voice steady and calm. "But attacking them would be equally reckless. The humans have resources and technology we can't match. If we escalate, they'll only respond with greater force."

A murmur of agreement rippled through the group, though some members remained visibly conflicted, their expressions a mix of anger and fear. After much discussion, the leaders agreed to intensify their surveillance and to establish a series of emergency protocols for each clan to follow in case the humans encroached too close.

The decision brought little comfort, but it was all they could do for now. Their unity, though tested, held strong under the pressure of a shared danger.

In the days that followed, the presence of humans in the forest grew more pronounced. The clans soon noticed that the humans had begun using even more sophisticated equipment—tracking devices, night-vision goggles, thermal imaging, and search dogs. Clearly, the humans now believed they were on the trail of something significant, something worth every ounce of effort.

Kora, who had gone on a scouting mission with Rina and Varo, witnessed one such patrol from a concealed perch high in the trees. The humans moved in organized formations, their voices low but purposeful as they followed a carefully mapped route.

"They're looking for something specific," Rina whispered, watching the humans as they moved below. "It's almost as if they're tracking us."

Varo clenched his fists, his face filled with frustration. "If they keep pushing, they'll eventually find us. We're running out of options."

The sight of the humans' relentless search filled them with a renewed urgency, and they returned to their clans with a growing sense of dread. The knowledge that the humans had increased their efforts created a tense atmosphere, each clan member acutely aware that a single mistake could bring disaster upon them all.

As the humans continued their push into the forest, the clans braced for the worst, each clan leader implementing strict routines to protect their members and prepare for an emergency escape if needed. They set up hidden routes deep into the forest, paths so twisted and concealed that only those who knew the terrain intimately could navigate them safely.

Erek, Varo, Rina, and Kora played a crucial role in coordinating these preparations, guiding members through the escape paths and drilling them on silent signals that would alert them if the humans drew too near. The focus on teamwork and trust helped ease the rising tension, each member knowing that their survival depended on the strength of their bonds.

Kora, watching her clan move through the routines with stoic determination, felt a swell of pride mixed with fear. "We may be few, but we're strong," she whispered to Varo, who stood beside her.

Varo took her hand, giving it a reassuring squeeze. "And together, we're unbreakable."

47

HOUNDS

The final escalation came on a foggy evening, when scouts from Stone Ridge and Riverbend, stationed along the forest's edge, spotted humans moving in a formation far closer than ever before. This time, they were equipped with search dogs, their powerful flashlights piercing through the darkness as they advanced in a relentless march.

Erek and Varo, alerted by a quick signal from the scouts, moved to the forest's edge, their hearts pounding as they realized how close the humans had come. The air was thick, each breath laden with the knowledge that a single misstep could reveal their presence.

One of the dogs caught a scent, and the humans turned, their flashlights aimed in the scouts' direction. Erek exchanged a look with Varo, their eyes filled with a shared understanding.

This was it. They had run out of time.

As they slipped back into the shadows to warn the others, a decision loomed over them, heavy and unavoidable. They could stay and risk discovery, hoping their defenses would hold, or they could abandon their sanctuary, journeying deeper into the wilderness in search of a new home beyond the reach of humans.

In that moment, they knew that whatever they chose, their lives would never be the same.

The days following Kaelan and Darek's encounter with the humans felt like an unwelcome awakening, the entire forest alive with the undercurrent of a restless pursuit. Erek and Varo, along with Rina and Kora, observed from a hidden ridge as the humans moved with renewed purpose, sweeping deeper into the heart of Stone Ridge and Riverbend territory. Each day, their numbers seemed to increase, new equipment, search dogs, and the hum of drones patrolling the skies.

Erek watched humans set up a camp near Stone Ridge's edge. Their voices carried across the clearing as they prepared for another day of searching, excited about finding something rare. To the humans, the forest was a mystery, but to the clans, it was a living home whose peace was being shattered.

"They're not slowing down," Varo said beside Erek, his eyes narrowed. "It's like they've caught a scent they can't let go of."

Erek nodded, his mind racing with possible solutions. The humans were close—too close—and every instinct told him that if something wasn't done soon, the entire territory would be compromised. He looked over at Rina and Kora, whose expressions mirrored his own sense of urgency.

"We have to warn the others," Erek said finally. "If they continue like this, it won't be long before they're pushing into every part of our territory."

"We can't handle this alone. And if it comes to it..." He hesitated, then continued, "We might have to face them directly."

Erek didn't answer, but the look in his eyes conveyed his understanding. They were standing on the precipice of something far bigger than a simple territorial dispute. If the humans continued their advance, confrontation was inevitable.

Later that evening, Erek gathered a small group from his new clan, calling over a young scout, Lira. She was one of the most skilled juveniles in Stone Ridge, swift and clever, and he knew she could deliver the message with precision and urgency.

"Lira, I need you to take a message to my mother," he began, his tone somber. "Omaki and the others are in the mountains. Tell her the humans have intensified their search. They've come dangerously close to our borders, and they're advancing with every passing day."

Lira nodded, her face a picture of determination as she absorbed the gravity of the task. "I'll reach them quickly, Erek," she promised. "They'll know by tomorrow."

He placed a hand on her shoulder, offering her a reassuring nod. "Be careful. Don't let the humans see you. Take the highest trails, the least-worn paths, and stay hidden."

With a final nod, Lira turned and slipped into the shadows, disappearing into the forest as she began her journey toward the mountains. Erek watched her go, a sense of foreboding settling over him. There was no certainty in the path ahead—only a faint hope that the message would reach his family in time.

48

MESSENGER

The sun had barely risen when Lira arrived at the edge of the high mountain cave where Omaki and her clan had taken refuge. Her arrival stirred the morning quiet, and within moments, Omaki, Kabota, Asha, and the rest of the clan had gathered around her, sensing that her unexpected visit was not casual.

Omaki's face grew tense as she listened to Lira's message, the news of the humans' persistence striking a nerve. They had thought themselves safe in these remote heights, far from the reach of human curiosity. But the sighting of Kaelan and Darek had rekindled the humans' search, their tenacity pushing them farther and farther into the wilderness.

"Erek wanted me to warn you," Lira concluded, her voice steady despite her fatigue. "He says the humans are getting closer by the day, and they're coming with more determination than ever."

Omaki exchanged a worried glance with Asha, her mind racing with possible plans. "We'll need to decide quickly," she said. "If they're closing in, we may have to prepare to move again—or worse, prepare to defend ourselves."

Adanowa, who had listened intently, felt a familiar anger stirring within him. Memories of his family's last days returned with a sharp clarity, his hatred for the humans mingling with a new resolve. He couldn't stand by while the clans he had come to respect faced such a threat. Rising, he approached Omaki, his voice low and filled with purpose.

"I'm going with her," he said, his gaze unwavering. "If the clans are in danger, I need to be there to help protect them. This isn't a threat we can ignore."

Omaki's expression softened as she met his gaze, recognizing the resolve in his eyes. She knew of his past, the pain he had endured at the hands of humans, and she understood his desire to stand with those who now faced a similar danger.

"You don't have to do this alone, Adanowa," she said gently. "But if you feel this is what you must do, then go with our blessing. Help them as you would help us."

With a final nod, Adanowa turned to Lira. "Lead the way."

As Adanowa and Lira began their descent, the gravity of his decision weighed on him. This was more than a matter of protecting the clans; it was a chance to confront the darkness that had haunted him for years. The loss of his family to human violence was a scar that had never healed, a wound that had festered as he watched his new family struggle to survive.

But his choice was more than anger. As he descended the mountain, he realized his return wasn't just for revenge, but to protect those he'd called his own. Lira led the way, navigating the rocky terrain easily. As they traversed narrow paths and descended through dense thickets, Adanowa's resolve strengthened. He'd learned from his past and wouldn't let these humans take another family from him.

"Almost there," Lira whispered as they neared the edge of Stone Ridge territory. The sight of familiar landmarks comforted Adanowa, reminding him that he was not alone in this fight.

The journey back to the clans' territory was fraught with tension. Every sound seemed amplified, each rustling leaf or distant call a reminder of the ever-present threat. Adanowa's eyes scanned the surroundings, his senses sharpened by years of survival. Memories of his family's last days flashed through his mind, but he pushed them aside, focusing instead on the task at hand.

As they descended further, he thought of Erek, Varo, and the others who would be waiting for his arrival. He knew his presence would bring them some comfort, a reassurance that they were not alone in facing the danger that loomed over them. But he also knew that this time, their survival might depend on more than just evasion. They might have to stand their ground.

Lira glanced back at him, her expression a mixture of respect and curiosity. "I've heard stories about you, Adanowa." "About what happened to your family."

Adanowa nodded, his voice quiet. "I was only a youngster then, but I learned that humans don't understand what they can't control. They'll stop at nothing to capture what they seek, and if they see us as a threat, they won't show mercy."

She held his gaze, the weight of his words settling over her. "Then we'll be ready, whatever it takes."

By the time they reached the main Stone Ridge gathering area, night had fallen, casting long shadows over the trees. Erek, Varo, Rina, Kora, and other clan members had assembled, their faces a mix of relief and apprehension as they welcomed Adanowa.

Erek approached him, clasping his arm in a gesture of solidarity. "I knew you'd come," he said, his voice filled with gratitude. "We're facing something we can't evade alone."

Adanowa nodded, his gaze sweeping over the assembled group. "Then we face it together. We'll protect our home and each other, whatever comes."

The clans spent the next hours discussing their strategy, coordinating defenses, and establishing signals for an evacuation if it became necessary. Adanowa and Varo led small groups to set up natural barriers, while Rina and Kora distributed supplies to ensure that everyone was prepared for the possibility of a prolonged stand.

As dawn approached, the clans were united in purpose, their

collective resolve solidified by adanowa's return. They had seen too much, lost too much, to allow fear to rule them. They would protect each other and their home, standing strong against a force that sought to dismantle their way of life.

49

TRACKED

The quiet of the early morning was filled with anticipation as they prepared for what lay ahead, their unity a powerful defense against the looming threat. And as the first light touched the trees, they braced themselves for whatever the day might bring, knowing that this time, they would not be driven from their land without a fight.

The day began with an unremarkable quiet, a typical foraging trip for the Stone Ridge juveniles Kaelan, Jarek, and Lira. Each had grown accustomed to gathering food and herbs, moving with ease among the familiar trees as they identified plants to bring back to the clan. Birds chirped overhead, and the soft crunch of leaves underfoot was almost rhythmic as they bent and reached, stuffing their satchels with roots and berries.

But the drone watching them was a disruption, a threat that lingered above, a technology they couldn't hear or sense, yet one that marked their every move. The high-tech device drifted like a dark shadow through the morning mist, its unblinking lens capturing their forms, broadcasting back their movements to the humans it served.

Jarek had been telling Kaelan a story, his voice quiet as they walked through a densely wooded area. Lira, with her keen senses, paused mid-step, glancing back as a flicker of movement above caught her eye. But the clouds covered the drone, and the disturbance went unnoticed, fading into the canopy of trees.

They laughed and whispered, unaware that their footprints, their faces, their every step were being recorded and tracked. By the time they reached the familiar markers of Stone Ridge territory, the drone had already locked onto their route and location, slipping away only after marking their final position.

Within minutes, the drone had returned to the human encampment, carrying with it the evidence needed to launch a calculated attack.

At the human command center below, a palpable energy filled the air as operatives studied the drone footage. Each screen showed the juveniles from Stone Ridge, their movements preserved in pixelated detail, their features etched onto the minds of the humans watching. They were no longer just rumors or mysterious figures—these were tangible, living beings. And for the humans who had spent weeks searching, this was a discovery worthy of celebration.

The lead operative, a man named Carson, addressed his team with a calm yet intense focus. "We have their location," he began, pointing to the screens. "This is the opportunity we've been waiting for. We'll move in quietly, and we'll take one alive if we can. Any resistance, neutralize it."

The operatives, clad in tactical gear and armed with tranquilizers, rifles, and tracking devices, moved in silence as they prepared. Their faces were set in determination, eyes cold and calculating. They didn't see their targets as beings with lives and families—they were simply rare specimens, worthy of capture.

The team deployed quickly, moving in pairs as they entered the forest with practiced ease, navigating trails and ridges as they closed in on the Stone Ridge clan. The mend women communicated through earpieces, their voices low, as they coordinated movements and double-checked the terrain. The only sound was the quiet hum of technology as their thermal imaging devices scanned the ground ahead, ensuring that no trace was left undetected.

The scout who returned to Stone Ridge brought an urgency that rippled through the clan like a wildfire. Members looked up from their tasks, children were ushered away, and the elders exchanged glances filled with worry as they processed the news: humans were approaching.

Erek's voice rang out, calm but forceful, as he gathered the clan together, explaining the situation in concise, urgent words. Rina stood beside him, her face pale but resolute. Her hand found Erek's as he spoke, their silent bond a source of strength amidst the rising fear.

"We need everyone's help," Erek declared, scanning the faces of his people. "Those who can fight, prepare yourselves. The rest, stay out of sight and watch over the young ones. We don't know what we're up against, but we'll protect our home, no matter what."

Kora joined Rina, gathering the young and elderly members, leading them to a hidden nook within the deeper part of the forest. She whispered soothing words to the children, assuring them that they were safe, her tone filled with a calm authority that belied the fear in her eyes.

In the gathering shadows, warriors from both Stone Ridge and Riverbend prepared in solemn silence, arming themselves with sharpened rocks and improvised weapons, knowing that these were no match for the humans' technology but resolved to fight nonetheless. Each clan member took a moment to look around, connecting with the family and friends who had become their lifeline, finding courage in the faces they had known their whole lives.

Adanowa was the last to join, stepping forward as the clans arranged themselves, his towering figure a steady presence. "This is our home," he said, his voice carrying through the trees. "And today, we fight for it."

The humans advanced with amazing precision, their eyes

sweeping over the undergrowth as they moved. Then, without warning, the first clash broke out.

A Stone Ridge scout hurled a rock that hit one of the mens helmet, sending him staggering back. It was the signal that ignited the battle. Members of Stone Ridge and Riverbend surged forward, their movements swift and calculated, using the thick trees for cover as they closed the distance.

Bullets cracked through the air, shattering the forest's tranquility. Bark splintered as rounds tore through the trees, sending shards scattering. Clan members darted forward, grabbing branches to disorient their enemies, ducking and weaving as they attempted to strike back with rocks and the occasional sharpened branch.

But the humans were prepared. They fired with brutal efficiency, targeting clan members who came too close, their tranquilizers mixed with lethal rounds as they strove to subdue the clans without wiping them out entirely. Some members fell, their bodies slumping as tranquilizers took effect, while others dropped silently to the ground, never to rise again.

In the midst of the chaos, Adanowa led a charge that struck fear into the humans, his powerful form breaking through their ranks as he swung a branch with a force that sent two of the intruders stumbling back. His roar was one of defiance, a challenge that resounded through the forest as he rallied his people.

Erek and Varo fought side by side, using every tactic they had learned to disrupt the human forces. They aimed to damage the humans' equipment, breaking equipment and seizing radios in a desperate attempt to throw them off balance.

But for every small victory, the clans suffered a loss. The sight of fallen friends, the cries of the wounded, tore at their spirits, yet they pressed on, unwilling to give an inch to the enemy that sought to destroy them.

Amidst the melee, Adanowa became the primary target. The humans, realizing his strength and leadership, deployed a strange looking weapon. A dart struck him in the shoulder, the sedative flooding his system.

Adanowa staggered, his vision swimming as he felt his strength drain away, his limbs growing heavy and unresponsive. He struggled to stay upright, his gaze meeting those of his fellow clan members as they continued to battle around him. He saw their desperation, their determination, and he felt the pain of failure as his knees hit the ground.

50

CAPTURE

The men moved in quickly, using a large piece of heavy equipment to clamp onto Adanowa's limp form, lifting him from the ground with an almost mechanical indifference. Clan members screamed in horror as they watched him, helpless, being lifted onto the back of a massive truck. He lay motionless, his vision darkening, the last sounds he heard the anguished cries of his people.

Varo, seeing Adanowa's capture, let out a primal scream and surged forward, heedless of his own safety. He swung at the humans, his strikes wild and desperate as he attempted to reach his fallen comrade. But a gunshot rang out, and Varo fell, a dark stain spreading across his chest as he collapsed to the ground.

Erek, witnessing Varo's fall, let out a strangled cry, running toward his brother's body, only to be held back by Rina, who clutched his arm in desperation. "Erek, no!" she shouted, her voice thick with grief.

The humans moved back, retreating as they secured their prize. They had what they came for, and as they withdrew, their faces were filled with a chilling satisfaction.

As the sounds of the humans' retreat faded, the clans emerged from the shadows, their expressions filled with shock and despair as they looked upon the battlefield. Bodies lay scattered across the ground, both wounded and dead, each a painful reminder of what they had sacrificed.

Erek knelt beside Varo, his hands shaking as he cradled his brother's lifeless body. His tears fell silently, each one a tribute to the memories they had shared, the dreams they had once harbored. Around him, clan members gathered in mourning, each weighed down by the enormity of their loss.

Rina, her face pale and eyes red-rimmed, knelt next to him. "He fought with everything he had," she whispered. "And so did Adanowa."

The clan members were left to grapple with their new reality. The strongest among them was gone, captured and taken away to an unknown fate. Their home had been desecrated, their people wounded, killed, and broken. But even as they mourned, a quiet determination began to take root, a resolve to continue, to survive, even in the face of overwhelming odds.

They knew now that the world had shifted, that their way of life had been irrevocably altered. The memory of Varo's sacrifice, of Adanowa's capture, would become the force that propelled them forward, uniting them in a common cause. And as they gathered the wounded and prepared to honor the fallen, they braced themselves for the path ahead, a path that would be dark and uncertain, but one they would face together.

The morning light was soft, filtering gently through the trees as Omaki, Asha, Kabota, and the others went about their daily tasks. A distant cry broke the peaceful silence, carrying with it a note of sorrow that sent a chill through Omaki's heart. She turned quickly, spotting a scout from the Stone Ridge clan making his way toward her, his face shadowed with grief.

Omaki's heart tightened as the scout approached, bearing the weight of news that felt heavier than words. His voice was a whisper, laden with sorrow. "Varo has fallen. And Adanowa... He was taken."

The grief spread through the group like a tangible wave, each member reacting in their own silent agony. Varo's loss struck them like a blow, a wound to the heart of their family, while the knowledge of Adanowa's capture filled them with dread. Varo had been a friend, a guide, a fierce protector, a son and to think of him gone seemed unthinkable.

Asha, her face tight with shock, took a breath as if to steady herself. "He was brave," she said, her eyes distant as she recalled moments spent with Varo, memories now edged with sorrow. "Always ready to stand up for us all."

Meika closed her eyes, a tear slipping down her cheek. "He was a light to us, even in the darkest moments. To think we've lost him... and that Adanowa may be suffering at their hands..."

Omaki, despite her own heart breaking, was determined to remain strong. "We must honor him, then. Varo deserves a farewell worthy of the life he gave to us."

The clan gathered in silence, preparing to make the journey to the sacred burial grounds, a place known only to the clans—a hidden, revered sanctuary where their ancestors rested, untouched by human eyes.

51

HONOR

Every member knew the path to the sacred site well, though it felt different on this day of mourning. Omaki and her clan moved with quiet purpose, each step a silent testament to their loss. As they walked, memories of Varo filled their hearts, his presence felt in the rustling leaves and cool breeze, as if he walked beside them one final time.

Omaki's thoughts drifted to moments with Varo, his easy laughter and unwavering strength. She remembered his patient guidance, his fierce loyalty, and the way he could calm even the wildest of tempers. These memories brought a bittersweet comfort, a reminder of the life he had lived, even as they faced the reality of his absence.

Kabota, walking close by, broke the silence with a quiet voice. "He protected us all, even when the cost was high. Varo was never one to let fear hold him back."

Omaki nodded, eyes downcast. "His strength is a part of us now, as it was always meant to be."

Raela, normally soft-spoken, shared her own memories. "Varo taught me to see the forest not just as a place to live, but as a place to feel and understand. His lessons were as constant as the trees, and I owe him so much of who I am."

Koda, his face marked by sorrow and frustration, clenched his fists as he walked. "We've lost so much to the humans. First our homes, and now... Varo. And Adanowa in their hands. It doesn't feel fair."

It isn't fair, Koda," Omaki said. "But we must carry on, carrying their strength with us. Today, we honor Varo's life and everything he stood for."

Their words hung in the air as they pressed onward, the journey transforming into a pilgrimage of remembrance, each step bringing them closer to a place that held their history, and now, would hold Varo's memory as well.

By dusk, the clans had gathered in the sacred burial grounds, an ancient grove encircled by towering trees. The air was heavy with reverence as members from Stone Ridge, Red Valley, Riverbend, Mistwood, and Omaki's own clan joined together, each finding their place around Varo's body, which lay wrapped in ceremonial hides and adorned with herbs and flowers carefully chosen to honor his spirit.

Omaki knelt beside Varo, her hand resting gently on his chest. She closed her eyes, whispering words of farewell, gratitude, and love, asking for his spirit to be safely guided to join their ancestors. Beside her stood Erek, his face pale, eyes filled with unshed tears as he struggled to find the strength to let go of his brother.

Marla, leader of the Red Valley clan, stepped forward, holding a bundle of cedar and sage. With steady hands, she lit the bundle, the fragrant smoke rising and swirling above Varo as she began a traditional chant. Her voice was strong and clear, a melody that spoke of protection, remembrance, and the eternal ties that bound their people together.

Jarok, the Stone Ridge leader, approached next, placing a stone by Varo's side—a symbol of strength and resilience, his words steady and filled with respect. "You were the rock among us, Varo. Your spirit will continue to guide us, and we will carry your strength in our hearts."

Tyrek, Riverbend's leader, took a feather and placed it beside Varo's hand. His voice was quiet, but there was a fierce loyalty in his gaze as he spoke. "You were the wind that moved us forward, Varo. Your courage was a flame that brightened our darkest days."

Lora, Mistwood's leader, moved forward last, her voice soft and reverent as she placed a woven leaf bracelet around Varo's wrist. "Your life was woven with ours, Varo. Though you are gone, your spirit remains with us, interwoven in the life we share."

One by one, each clan member approached to pay their respects, offering small tokens of remembrance—a stone, a flower, a whispered prayer. The air grew thick with sorrow and reverence as Varo's loved ones honored his spirit, his sacrifice.

Finally, Erek knelt beside his brother, his hands trembling as he placed a woven leaf on Varo's chest. "I don't know how to say goodbye," he said, his voice breaking. "But I promise I'll live my life to honor yours, Varo. I'll protect our people, our home, and I'll carry everything you taught me."

With a final whisper, Erek bowed his head, and the clans fell silent as they laid Varo to rest, returning him to the sacred ground of his ancestors.

Once the burial was complete, the leaders gathered on the edge of the clearing, their faces solemn as they prepared to discuss what lay ahead. Jarok from Stone Ridge, Marla from Red Valley, Tyrek from Riverbend, and Lora from Mistwood joined Omaki, each carrying the weight of their people's hopes, fears, and unspoken grief.

Jarok, his voice a low rumble, began the conversation. "This cannot go on as it has. The humans grow bolder with every sighting, and now we've lost Varo and Adanowa. If we stay here, we risk everything."

Marla, known for her fierce protectiveness of Red Valley, shook her head. "And where would we go, Jarok? The humans expand their reach daily. No place in these lands is untouched by them. If we flee, it may only postpone the threat, not end it."

Tyrek, his face clouded with doubt, added, "But if we fight, we risk more lives. Varo is gone, and Adanowa... Who knows what horrors he may face in their hands. Is there a way to stay hidden, to avoid their sight entirely?"

Lora's voice was thoughtful, filled with a sorrowful wisdom. "We could try to live more as shadows, using our knowledge of the land to blend with it, to avoid detection. It's a difficult life, but perhaps it's our best hope if we are to remain in these lands."

Omaki listened as each leader shared their thoughts, her own heart weighed down by the grief of losing her son and her mate, her mind racing with the knowledge of what staying or leaving would mean for her people. She had guided them through many trials, but now, faced with the relentless human threat, even she was uncertain.

"We cannot live forever in fear," she said softly. "But we must also face reality. If we stay, we must become more vigilant, more cautious than ever. But if we leave... we must be certain it's to a place they cannot find."

Erek, standing nearby, stepped forward, his voice calm but filled with pain. "Varo wouldn't want us to run in fear. He believed in standing strong, in protecting what we have. We owe it to him to find a way to keep our home and our people safe."

The leaders exchanged glances, each weighing the risks, the sacrifices, the painful choices that lay before them. Whatever decision they made, it would change the fabric of their lives, testing the strength of their bonds and their ability to protect each other in a world that seemed determined to tear them apart.

As dawn began to break, casting a gentle light over the clearing, the clans gathered once more, each leader offering a silent nod of respect to one another as they prepared to return to their respective territories. The bonds formed during the ceremony felt stronger than ever, binding them in a shared grief and a resolve to honor Varo's memory.

Omaki held Erek close, her heart heavy as she whispered to him, "Varo's spirit lives in you, Erek. Carry it with you, let it guide you. And know that you're never alone."

Erek nodded, his face resolute even as his heart ached. "I'll make him proud, Mother. I promise you that."

Each clan member bid their farewells, moving with a sense of purpose and solidarity as they turned away from the sacred site. They carried with them the strength of their ancestors, the memory of Varo's sacrifice, and the spirit of unity that bound them to each other.

As they disappeared into the forest, the silence of the sacred burial grounds remained, a solemn witness to the vows made and the resolve strengthened. They would face the coming days with courage, united by loss, resilience, and the spirit of those who had gone before them.

PART IV

52

SPRING

The arrival of spring swept through the forest, bringing the familiar scents of fresh pine and blooming wildflowers. Sunlight filtered through the budding leaves, and the streams surged with melted snow, filling the air with a soft, constant hum. Koda, now seven, darted between the trees, his energy boundless as he explored, picking up stones and marveling at the fresh blossoms that painted the forest floor.

Omaki watched him with a mixture of pride and sadness, knowing that this forest, this mountain they had called home through the winter, would soon be left behind. Her heart weighed heavy with memories of Adanowa and Varo, whose sacrifices had enabled them to survive. But she was resolute; to give Koda and the young ones a chance at a safer life, they had to go east, away from the reach of human eyes.

She felt someone behind her and turned to see Kabota, his gaze filled with understanding. "The mountains have sheltered us," he said, as if reading her thoughts, "but it's time we sought a place humans do not know—a place Koda and the others can grow without fear."

Omaki nodded, the strength in his words steadying her. "I've thought of nothing else," she replied. "Our family deserves peace, and perhaps we'll find it there."

As Koda ran up to them, proudly showing a stone he'd found, Omaki's heart softened. She knelt beside him. "We're going on a journey soon, Koda," she said gently. "Farther than you've ever gone before."

Koda's eyes widened with excitement. "Will there be more forests? New animals?"

Omaki smiled, placing a hand over his. "Yes, little one. We'll find new places and make them our own."

Two days later, the leaders of the five clans gathered in a quiet, secluded grove near Stone Ridge territory. Omaki of the Hoh Clan arrived with Kabota, Asha, Koda, Raela and Meika by her side, while the others, led by Jarok of Stone Ridge, Marla of Red Valley, Tyrek of Riverbend, and Lora of Mistwood, took their places in the circle. Each leader's expression was marked by a somber determination; the weight of recent losses lingered like a shadow over them all.

The silence that begins the meeting is somber, and each leader seems reluctant to speak first, feeling the weight of responsibility to their clans. Finally, Tyrek steps forward.

"We cannot ignore the truth," he begins, his voice steady but filled with tension. "The humans have seen us, hunted us. Adanowa is gone, and Varo..." He pauses, visibly struggling with his emotions before continuing. "The humans are dangerous, and they're relentless. If they could track us here, what's to stop them from returning?"

Omaki nods slowly, her gaze shifting to meet Tyrek's. "It's true, Tyrek. We've lost so much, and every moment we remain risks more loss." Her voice grows softer. "But there is more to this than just survival. This is our home. The lands our ancestors protected, where our young ones learn to thrive." She looks over to Koda, standing beside her, his young face filled with worry and determination. "Leaving means abandoning that."

Jorok, who had been listening in silence, speaks up, his voice deep and commanding. "Omaki, I hear you. But as much as I wish it weren't true, Tyrek is right. We've been here for generations, and humans have always known of us, sensed us even if they hadn't yet seen us. But now... this is different. They've taken one of our own."

The clan members shift, nodding to show their agreement. They remember the day Adanowa was taken, his strength drained by human weaponry, his capture witnessed with horror. His absence has left a void that none can ignore.

From the edges of the gathering, a voice rises. It's Raela, a younger member of the Hoh Clan, her voice edged with anger. "And what's to say that it would be any different anywhere else?" she asks, her tone bold. "We move east or north, maybe even deeper into the mountains, but what happens when the humans come there too? Will we keep running?"

Raela's words hang heavy in the air, and a tone of agreement echoes from some of the younger clan members. They are weary of hiding, weary of abandoning places that feel like home.

Omaki turns to her, her expression a mix of sadness and understanding. "You're right, Raela. There's no promise that moving will give us peace. The humans are expanding their reach, searching in places they never dared to go. But if staying means more lives lost, is it not worth considering? If moving could spare us, even for a time, is that not a chance we should take?"

Raela frowns, her fists clenched at her sides. "But our strength lies in knowing this land. The caves, the rivers, the trees—they're all part of us. We leave, and we become strangers, always on the edge of survival."

Marla, the Red Valley leader, raises a hand to silence the others, her voice calm yet filled with the wisdom of experience. "Raela makes a fair point," she says. "Our ancestors chose these lands because they offered protection. We are hidden here, and if we move to new lands, we may be vulnerable, unfamiliar with what dangers lie there. Moving could place us at greater risk."

Tyrek shakes his head, his expression pained. "Greater risk than what, Marla? We've already seen what they can do. If the humans know our ways, there's no telling how long before they track us here again."

Each member of the clans remembers the human machines—the drones, the firearms, and even stranger devices that emit sounds and lights designed to disorient them. Those who were near during the attacks had witnessed first-hand the humans' cruelty, and fear simmers in their eyes as they recall that day.

Lora steps forward, her presence calming the crowd. "There is truth on both sides. Leaving feels like a defeat, but staying could mean another tragedy. I believe we owe it to ourselves to weigh both choices. If we stay, we risk another encounter with the humans, but we retain the advantage of knowing the land. If we leave, it must be to a place so remote that not even the humans can reach us."

The conversation grows more intense, with each clan leader contributing their perspective. Jorok, who had initially sided with staying, begins to see the sense in Tyrek's argument.

"Lora," he says, nodding respectfully, "I hear your wisdom. A new territory could offer safety, but where could we find such a place? We would be abandoning our defenses, our familiarity, for an unknown land." He hesitates, torn. "But perhaps... there's strength in numbers. If all our clans went together, we might be able to survive in a place no human would dare to go."

Omaki watches the leaders, her heart heavy with the realization that the decision might mean dividing the clans. She looks to Koda, Kabota, Asha and the younger ones watching in silence, their futures uncertain. A fierce resolve fills her, and she addresses the clans.

"We cannot let fear drive us," she begins. "But we must also acknowledge that we're no longer hidden here. We've lost Adanowa, Varo, and others to this struggle. If moving east, deeper into unknown territories, could give us even a few seasons of peace, it's worth trying." Her eyes meet each leader's. "I would rather see our young ones grow up free than live in the constant shadow of fear."

The silence that follows is thoughtful, the clans absorbing Omaki's words. Some in agreement, and others remain uncertain, but the tension slowly shifts into a sense of resolution.

Marla speaks again, her tone more conciliatory. "Perhaps... Perhaps those of us who wish to stay can hold this land, guarding it in the event we ever need to return. The others could seek a safer home to the east, one far removed from human paths."

Lora nods. "This way, we remain unified even if we are not physically together. Those who go may find a new land for us all, and those who stay may protect the memory of those we've lost."

Omaki feels a surge of gratitude for Marla and Lora's willingness to consider both paths. This compromise could mean that her clan, the Hoh, might venture east in search of a safer land, while the others maintain their presence in the mountains, ensuring that the legacy of their territory is not entirely lost.

Tyrek adds his voice, nodding to Omaki. "Then it's decided. We'll part ways for now, some to remain and some to seek a new home. But our bond as clans will not be broken. We will stay in contact and come to one another's aid if ever needed."

Jorok steps forward. "We will protect this place, Omaki, and if your clan finds a new haven, you will always have our support."

The meeting concluded, and the clans gathered to bid farewell to those leaving. The Hoh Clan, joined by Tyrek's Riverbend and Lora's Mistwood, prepared for the journey. Omaki, Kabota, Asha, Meika, Raela, Paka, and young Koda stood together.

Omaki embraced Jarok. "Thank you for standing by us. I wish you strength, Jarok, and peace in the high places you will call home."

Jarok nodded, his gaze filled with respect. "And to you, Omaki. May you find the peace you seek in the east, and know you have friends here always."

Marla stepped forward, taking Omaki's hands. "You carry the hopes of all of us with you. May your journey be safe, and may we meet again one day."

Tyrek, standing with Lora, took a deep breath, his voice firm. "We will travel with you, Omaki. Together, we will find new places, a home beyond the reach of the humans."

53

RESOLVE

With one last look at the mountains that had sheltered them for so long, Omaki gathered her clan, a mixture of hope and sorrow filling her heart. They had shared so much with these clans, and though their paths diverged, she knew their bond would remain strong.

As the sun set, casting a golden light over the forest, the Hoh, Riverbend, and Mistwood clans began their journey eastward, each step taking them farther from the familiar and closer to an unknown future. The memories of those they had lost guided them, a constant presence that reminded them of the strength that lay within.

The clans moved quietly, the Olympic Peninsula shrouded in the familiar hush of morning fog. Trees towered over them, their branches stretching skyward like sentries watching over their departure. Omaki, standing with Koda by her side, took one last, solemn look at the landscape that had been their home for generations.

The young ones, like Koda, Raela, and Paka, wore expressions of excitement and worry. For them, the forest was as familiar as the faces of their family; leaving it felt like losing a part of themselves. Omaki, who carried the weight of their ancestors' legacy, turned to her people. "We go forward to find a new place, a place beyond the reach of humans. But no matter where we go, the spirit of these forests will be with us."

With these words, the clans moved eastward, leaving behind the coastal pines, cold beaches, and memories of those they had lost. Kabota and Tyrek led the way, with Lora and her Mistwood clan walking close behind. The terrain was dense, the trees getting thicker as they climbed toward the Cascade Range. Each step away from the coast felt like leaving behind pieces of themselves, but necessity drove them onward.

By the time they reached the foothills of the Cascades, exhaustion was weighing on the clans. The rugged terrain forced them to move slowly, climbing steep inclines and navigating narrow paths surrounded by thorny underbrush. With every movement, they took care to avoid leaving tracks, erasing footprints in soft mud and brushing away bent foliage. Staying hidden required constant vigilance, especially in the presence of human trails and logging roads that cut through the woods like veins.

Omaki's sharp eyes scanned the surroundings, noting every movement. A rustle to her left turned out to be a family of deer, but she kept her guard up. The Cascades were alive with creatures more dangerous than deer—wolves, mountain lions, and bears were known to patrol the area, and even the scent of a sasquatch clan could provoke these predators.

One night, as they set up a temporary camp near a freshwater stream, Kabota heard distant howls echoing through the trees. Wolves. He motioned to Tyrek and Omaki, signaling the need for silence. The wolves' howls grew closer, but the clans remained hidden, camouflaged in the thick underbrush. Hours passed before the wolves moved on, their calls fading into the distance. Omaki's listened to the stillness return, grateful they hadn't been discovered.

The clans faced hunger too. The mountain vegetation was unfamiliar, and edible plants were scarce. They relied on Kabota's knowledge to find roots and berries, but their reserves grew thin, and the clans' strength waned. Moving quietly through the mountains required energy, and with food hard to come by, tempers began to fray. The elders took less food to save rations for the young, but Omaki noticed the toll it was taking on everyone.

They traveled mostly by night, a tactic that kept them hidden but increased the risk of stumbling across human settlements or campers. As they skirted close to a small logging camp one night, the glow of firelight and the smell of cooked meat drifted through the trees. Koda tugged on Omaki's arm, his eyes wide with hunger, and she gently pulled him back, her heart heavy.

"Soon, Koda," she whispered, "we'll find a place where we can rest and eat."

After days of traversing the rugged Cascades, the clans finally descended into the high plains, leaving behind the safety of forest cover. Here, the landscape stretched into vast open fields and rolling hills, where trees grew sparsely, and shelter was difficult to find. Staying hidden became a greater challenge.

The clans were forced to travel under the cover of darkness and huddle in tall grasses during the day. The winds were strong, and though they masked scents, they also carried the risk of exposure. Jorok grumbled at the constant wind, his eyes narrowed as he scanned the horizon. "We're as exposed as prey here," he said. "If a human were to look, they'd see us clear as day."

The lack of shelter made it difficult to rest, and the clans moved with a weariness that grew heavier each day. Food was even scarcer here; they relied on finding small game, such as rabbits or prairie dogs, which they hunted carefully, ensuring not to leave behind any blood or remnants that could attract predators—or worse, humans.

One night, as they crossed a field, they heard the roar of an approaching vehicle—a truck, its headlights slicing through the darkness. Omaki motioned for silence, and the clans dropped to the ground, remaining still as the truck rumbled past. They stayed that way long after it disappeared, knowing that one wrong move in these open plains could cost them dearly.

After weeks of exposed travel, the clans reached the dense forests of the Midwest. Here, the trees stood tall and close, offering a sanctuary of sorts but with new challenges. The region was filled with human recreation areas, from campsites to hiking trails, and the clans had to navigate cautiously. The smell of campfire smoke and the faint sounds of voices frequently reminded them of the humans who ventured into these woods.

One evening, as the clans passed through a thickly wooded area, they encountered a small group of campers. The humans were laughing and unaware of the silent figures watching from the shadows. But a crackling sound—a branch breaking underfoot—alerted one of the humans, who froze and glanced around, flashlight in hand.

"Did you hear that?" the human whispered, scanning the darkness.

Omaki held her breath, motioning for everyone to stay perfectly still. The human shone their light through the trees, pausing near where Koda crouched behind a log, barely concealed. After what felt like an eternity, the human shrugged and returned to their campfire, unaware of the eyes watching them.

The clans moved swiftly, putting as much distance as possible between themselves and the campsite. But this incident served as a reminder that the wilderness, though familiar, was never completely safe from human presence.

After months of travel, the clans reached the rugged terrain of the Appalachian Mountains. Although the thick forests and valleys provided more shelter, they encountered new dangers. The Appalachian trails were popular with hunters and hikers, and it was not uncommon to see drones or hear the distant crack of gunshots.

They carefully avoided marked trails, moving through ravines and shadowed forests, relying on Kabota and Tyrek's knowledge of survival tactics to stay hidden. The mountains, however, were challenging; steep inclines and rocky ground made the journey physically taxing, and the clan members grew weaker with each passing day.

One night, as they navigated a narrow cliffside path, a drone buzzed overhead, its bright lights sweeping the area. Omaki ordered everyone to freeze, crouching low among the rocks. The drone passed, but their fear lingered. They were close to their destination, but the danger had only intensified.

54

HOPE

Finally, they began to see changes in the landscape. The forest canopy thickened, and the ground softened underfoot as they neared North Carolina. The mist-laden mountains, reminiscent of their homeland, gave them hope. The clans shared quiet conversations about rebuilding, of resting, of finding a place where they might live without constant fear.

As they approached what would become their new sanctuary, a feeling of unity filled them. They had faced hunger, exhaustion, and the unrelenting presence of humans. They had traveled far, but they had endured together.

Omaki looked around at her people—Tyrek, Kabota, Lora, and the young ones, including Koda. They had lost much but had gained resilience. And as they stepped into their new land, they felt the weight of their journey lift, replaced by the hope of a fresh start, a place where they could live in peace and honor the memory of those who had sacrificed to protect them.

As they began to explore the area, they found a series of caves carved into the hillsides, tucked behind dense thickets and surrounded by tall pines and ancient oaks. The caves were cool and deep, and large enough to provide shelter for all three clans. There were even smaller side caverns, perfect for storage or quiet spaces where clan members could retreat. For Omaki and the other leaders, this network of caves was a discovery that seemed almost too perfect, like an answer to the quiet prayers they had sent into the wind during their journey.

The nearby forests offered more than just shelter. Rivers criss-crossed through the valleys, clear and cold, their waters rich with fish and the banks covered in edible plants. There were signs of deer, wild turkeys, and smaller game, the kind that could sustain the clans through the seasons if they hunted carefully and respectfully. The towering trees of this land were a familiar sight, and the mossy ground, dense undergrowth, and fragrant pine needles brought a feeling of comfort to the weary travelers.

Omaki watched as the younger members of the clans, Koda included, marveled at the forest, their earlier exhaustion melting away. The elders seemed relieved as well, their shoulders relaxing as they touched the trees and breathed the fresh mountain air. It was as if they had found a new sanctuary.

But as they explored, they soon realized that this land, while secluded, was not as isolated as they had hoped.

While surveying the land's boundaries, Kabota and Tyrek discovered something—a narrow dirt road, rutted from years of wear, winding along the edge of their territory. They followed it cautiously until they spotted a few cabins nestled between the trees, smoke wafting from the chimneys and lights flickering through the windows. These homes were distant enough that the humans hadn't noticed the clans' arrival, but close enough to raise concern.

When Kabota reported back, unease spread through the clans. They had traveled for months, through dangerous terrain and near-starvation, seeking a place free from the threat of human presence. The sight of those remote homes so close to what they had hoped would be their sanctuary felt like a broken promise to some.

"It's no different than where we came from," one of the younger members of the Riverbend clan exclaimed, frustration and exhaustion coloring his voice. "We've spent our lives hiding from humans. And now, after all this... we're back where we started."

Others spoke in agreement, their discontent simmering. Even Lora, leader of the Mistwood clan, expressed her concern. The memory of Adanowa's capture and Varo's death was still raw, and fear of another attack lingered in everyone's hearts.

"Perhaps we went the wrong way," said another clan member. "Maybe we should have kept going, searched for somewhere truly wild."

But Omaki, Kabota, and Asha remained calm. Omaki watched the growing tension among her people, then glanced at Kabota and gave him a nod. It was time for them to remember why they had come here—and what they were searching for.

Kabota stepped forward, his gaze steady and thoughtful as he looked around at his family, his clan. His voice was deep and calm.

"Yes, there are humans nearby. I saw the cabins myself. But these people... They are not like those who hunt us in the forests or capture us with drones and weapons." He paused, letting his words sink in. "These are humans who live quietly, far from the noise and chaos of the cities. They are not here to search for us. They are here because they, too, have chosen a life away from others."

The clans listened, some crossing their arms, others nodding as they processed his words. Kabota continued, his voice carrying both strength and understanding.

"We have always lived alongside humans. On the Olympic Peninsula, we shared the land, and we did so by staying hidden, by watching from afar. Not all humans are like the ones who came with weapons and machines. Many do not even know we exist."

"But can we trust them?" someone asked from the back of the gathering. "How do we know they won't come looking for us once they see signs of our presence?"

Kabota gave a slight nod, acknowledging the fear in their question. "We don't know for sure. But we do know that humans come in many kinds. And I believe we owe it to ourselves, after all we've sacrificed, to give this place a chance."

Omaki could see that Kabota's words were calming the group, but not completely. The uncertainty was too fresh, and the scars of their recent losses ran too deep.

Asha, wise and thoughtful, stepped forward next. She had always been a quiet presence in the Hoh Clan, known for her insight and understanding of the old ways, and the clan members listened attentively as she spoke.

"In all my years, I have learned that balance comes from understanding, not from fear. Yes, we have been harmed by humans, but we have also been left alone by many of them. Even in our own lands, we have watched humans who go about their lives, who respect the forest, who are as afraid of the unknown as we are of them."

Her voice was gentle, like a breeze moving through the trees, but it held an undeniable strength. "These humans, here in this land, have chosen solitude just as we have. It may be that they want to be left alone as much as we do."

The clans shifted, considering her words. Asha's perspective carried a weight of experience, and her wisdom had guided the Hoh Clan through many challenges.

"Are we to fear all humans for the actions of some?" Asha asked quietly. "Or can we learn to live with them, as we always have—keeping ourselves safe, yes, but not living in fear of them?"

Her words struck a chord, and the tension in the air began to soften. The clans were beginning to see that not all humans posed a threat. But still, the hesitation lingered.

Omaki took a deep breath, stepping forward to address the clans. Her gaze was steady as she looked out at the faces of those she loved, those she had led on this difficult journey.

"Long ago, before our clans were divided by these mountains, our people lived in harmony with the native tribes who respected the forest. My ancestors taught me stories of how they would watch the Native American tribes from a distance, learning their ways, understanding their respect for the land."

She continued, her voice warming as she remembered the stories passed down from her own elders. "The humans who lived in those times were not so different from us. They honored the same land and took only what they needed. Our ancestors shared an unspoken understanding with them. There were times when a human and a sasquatch would cross paths, and they would part peacefully, respecting the space they shared."

Omaki paused, her gaze moving from face to face, seeing the doubt in some eyes but the growing understanding in others. "Just as we coexisted then, we may learn to coexist now. The humans nearby may see us, but we have always been shadows, hidden from the eyes of those who would harm us. We can be cautious, yes, but let us not forget the wisdom of our ancestors."

Omaki saw that the younger members of the clans, those who had grown up knowing only the fear of humans, were starting to soften. Koda looked up at her, his young eyes filled with hope and curiosity.

"So... we don't have to be afraid?" he asked.

Omaki knelt beside him. "No, Koda. We don't have to be afraid. But we must be wise. We will watch these humans, and if they show us respect, we will leave them in peace."

After a long discussion, the clans began to reach a consensus. The leaders of the Riverbend and Mistwood clans spoke with Omaki, Kabota, and Asha, sharing their thoughts and weighing the risks and benefits. They knew they had found a place rich with resources, a land that could sustain them, but it would take understanding and patience.

"We will stay," Tyrek finally said, his voice strong and resolved. "But we will remain vigilant. This land holds promise, and we must protect it. If the humans show signs of intrusion, we will act as needed, but until then, we will give them the benefit of the doubt."

Lora from Mistwood nodded in agreement. "We cannot keep running. If this is to be our home, then we must defend it and trust ourselves to find a way to live here."

The decision was made. The clans would establish their new sanctuary, using the caves as their base and spreading out through the surrounding forest. They would be cautious, watching for signs of human activity, but they would not let fear drive them from what could be the refuge they had long sought.

55

HOME

With their decision to stay solidified, the clans began setting up their new home. The caves offered ample space, and each clan took sections of the caverns for their own needs. The Hoh Clan chose a series of interconnected chambers near a clear, shallow stream that trickled through the cave floor, providing fresh water. The Riverbend Clan took the upper caverns with higher entrances, allowing them to keep watch over the territory, while Mistwood claimed the deeper caves, where the air was cool and the light was dim.

As the clans settled in, they felt a sense of calm. The forest was alive with sounds—birds singing, leaves rustling in the wind, and the occasional rustle of deer moving through the undergrowth. It was a comforting reminder of the wilderness they had fought so hard to reach.

Omaki and Kabota set about teaching the younger ones how to remain hidden, using shadows and natural cover to avoid being seen. Asha taught them to recognize the tracks of humans, distinguishing them from the natural trails created by animals, so they could sense intrusions long before they became a danger.

In the evenings, as the clans gathered to share stories, Omaki saw their spirits lifting. They were beginning to feel like a community again, like the sasquatch of old who had coexisted with the land and its inhabitants. She knew that the future held uncertainties, but for the first time since they had left the Olympic Peninsula, she felt a spark of hope.

The clans remained cautious, keeping a low profile and observing the distant cabin from afar. True to Kabota and Asha's predictions, the humans seemed to lead quiet lives, coming and going without venturing too deeply into the woods. There were a few tense moments—a wayward hunter crossing their territory, a curious hiker approaching the caves—but the clans stayed hidden, evading detection by slipping silently through the trees.

Koda and the young ones, under Omaki's watchful eye, learned to sense the humans' presence without fear. The clans adapted, each one finding their place in the rhythm of the forest. And as the weeks passed, they began to feel a cautious comfort, the sensation of belonging that had been absent for so long.

Omaki knew they would always need to be vigilant, that the humans could never truly be trusted. But as the clans settled into their new sanctuary, she felt confident that they had found a place where they could live, a place where they could remember those they had lost and build a future for those who would come after them.

As the sun set over the Appalachian mountains, casting golden light over the forest, Omaki looked out from the mouth of their cave, a deep sense of peace settling within her. They had endured, and now, they would thrive—together, as they had always done.

In the days following their arrival, the clans had begun to settle into their new sanctuary. But even as they adapted to this land, the clans remained wary of the few human dwellings scattered around the forest's edge. And though they had resolved to coexist cautiously, there remained an undercurrent of curiosity about the nearest homestead—the small house nestled in the middle of eighty forested acres, the closest sign of human life to their new home.

Omaki, Kabota, and Asha had discussed the homestead in careful, hushed tones. The clan leaders had observed the property from a distance but had refrained from exploring farther, still haunted by memories of the humans who had hunted and captured their own. But Kabota and Asha sensed that knowing more about these humans could offer valuable insight. If they were going to coexist, they needed to understand who they were living near.

After another quiet conversation with Omaki, the pair prepared to set out, agreeing to travel in silence and return before dawn. As they moved toward the homestead, slipping through the shadows of the dense forest, they were determined to blend into the landscape, keeping their presence concealed.

The homestead appeared through the trees, a modest wooden structure surrounded by a wire fence. The land was a mix of open space and tree cover, with patches of wild grass, a small vegetable garden, and a chicken coop off to one side. The early evening light cast a warm glow over the scene, making the place look peaceful.

Kabota and Asha crouched behind a dense thicket, observing the area with keen eyes. They spotted a small flock of chickens pecking around the fenced coop and a pair of goats grazing nearby, occasionally bleating to one another. Alongside the goats, they noticed three donkeys roaming the perimeter of the property, seemingly acting as protectors, an added layer of defense against predators.

The farmhouse itself was quaint and sturdy, with a small porch where two people—a man and a woman—sat talking, their voices carrying softly through the air. But it wasn't the adults who caught Asha's attention. Near the garden, she noticed a boy, perhaps twelve years old, moving between the plants with quiet focus, checking for ripe vegetables. She nudged Kabota and nodded toward the boy.

"Look there," she whispered. "He's young. This family... they seem different."

Kabota studied the scene, his expression thoughtful. He had seen the brutal side of humanity, but something about this place felt different. These humans lived simply, surrounded by animals and reliant on their land, a life of patience rather than violence.

"They're farmers," he said. "They're not here for us. Look at how they live—peaceful, quiet." He watched as the boy laughed at one of the goats who had wandered too close to the garden, shooing it back with a gentle nudge. "If we remain unseen, I don't think they'll be a threat."

As night began to settle, Kabota and Asha crept a little closer to the edge of the property, watching the animals and the boy who moved among them. The goats, with their calm, curious eyes, trotted along the fenced area, occasionally glancing toward the forest but more interested in grazing. The donkeys, however, were more alert, keeping their ears perked and occasionally braying if they sensed movement.

The boy appeared comfortable and skilled with the animals, moving between the goats and the chickens as he tended to his chores. At one point, he turned toward the forest, and Kabota and Asha instinctively froze. The boy's eyes searched the tree line, his face curious but not afraid. He stayed there for a moment, as if he sensed something in the shadows, before shrugging and returning to his work.

To the boy, they would be nothing more than a trick of the eye, shadows in the woods—a presence both invisible and silent.

"Do you think he knows?" Asha asked softly.

Kabota shook his head, a slight smile tugging at the corners of his mouth. "He's curious, but he doesn't know. To him, we're only part of the forest." He studied the boy's face, noting the innocence in his gaze. "It's a good thing. Innocence is rare in their kind."

They watched in silence as the boy completed his chores, finally heading inside with a small basket of vegetables. Once he had disappeared into the house, Asha and Kabota returned their focus to the homestead, making careful observations of the property layout and the family's routines.

Kabota and Asha spent the next several hours moving silently along the perimeter of the property, studying the family's daily routines and the layout of the homestead. They noted the locations of the chicken coop, the goat pen, and the donkeys' favorite grazing spots, learning the patterns that governed the animals' behavior. As they circled the house, they remained hyper-aware of any potential threats the property might pose to their clans.

The homestead seemed relatively unprotected by human standards. There were no lights that suggested security cameras, no guard dogs, and little to indicate that the humans feared intrusion. The donkeys patrolled the edges of the goat pen and the chicken coop, braying and stamping whenever something disturbed them, but otherwise, the farm was quiet.

Asha, however, was careful not to let her guard down. "If they were to discover us," she said, "they could still be a threat. Humans are unpredictable. Even those who live peacefully can be dangerous if frightened."

Kabota nodded, understanding her concern. "We'll continue to observe, but for now, it appears they're focused on their land, not the forest beyond."

With each passing moment, the farm seemed less threatening and more like a relic of a quieter, older way of life. These humans, though close by, might not need to be a source of worry if the clans were careful.

Just as they were preparing to leave, the boy reappeared on the porch, a small flashlight in hand. He walked slowly down the steps, shining the light in front of him, and wandered toward the edge of the yard. Kabota and Asha instinctively moved deeper into the shadows, careful to stay hidden.

The boy paused, scanning the tree line with his light. His gaze lingered on the exact spot where Asha crouched, her silhouette blending with the forest shadows. Kabota tensed, prepared to draw his companion back, but Asha remained motionless, her breath steady and controlled.

"Are you out there?" the boy whispered, his voice soft but clear in the night air. His question hung in the silence, almost as if he sensed a presence nearby. Kabota and Asha exchanged a glance, neither daring to move, waiting for the boy to turn back toward the house.

After a long pause, the boy sighed, lowering his flashlight. "If you're there... I won't tell anyone," he said. With one last look at the trees, he turned and made his way back to the house, leaving the forest silent once more.

When he was safely inside, Kabota exhaled, relief washing over him. "He sensed us," he whispered. "But he didn't seem afraid."

Asha nodded thoughtfully. "He's young. Children often sense things adults cannot. But he chose to leave us be." Her gaze softened as she considered the boy's words. "Perhaps there is no harm in this family after all."

Kabota and Asha returned to the clans just before dawn, their minds buzzing with the night's discoveries. They gathered the clan leaders—Omaki, Tyrek, and Lora—to share what they had seen, describing the family's peaceful routines and the boy's apparent innocence.

"This family... They live off the land, quietly," Kabota began. "They're not like the others we've known. The boy, he sensed our presence but wasn't afraid. He even spoke to us—almost as if he knew we were there."

Omaki listened carefully, her expression thoughtful. "Then he has the awareness that only a few humans possess," she said. "Some of them, the ones with open minds, can sense us without needing to see. But if he is unafraid, that speaks to their nature."

Tyrek, however, was more cautious. "That may be true, but what if they do see us? What if curiosity or fear drives them to seek us out? We can't let our guard down."

Asha nodded, understanding his concern. "We won't. We'll remain hidden, careful. But I believe there's no reason to fear this family. They're not like those who hunt us with weapons."

Lora leaned forward, her voice quiet but certain. "Perhaps they are the sort of humans Omaki spoke of—the ones who live in balance with the land. If we watch them closely, we might find that coexistence here is possible."

After much discussion, the clans agreed to remain cautious but hopeful, continuing to monitor the homestead without initiating contact. They would watch from the shadows, learning from these humans, just as they had done in times long past.

In the days that followed, Omaki found herself reflecting on Kabota and Asha's observations, considering the boy's innocence and the family's gentle way of life. As the clans continued to settle into their new home, she felt a growing curiosity about the humans, a sense that perhaps, in this land, coexistence might indeed be possible.

Omaki began sharing stories with the younger members of the clan, recounting the wisdom of their ancestors who had lived peacefully alongside indigenous humans in the past. She reminded them that not all humans sought to harm them, that some had chosen to protect the forest just as fiercely as they did.

Koda listened with wide eyes, his curiosity piqued. "So... we don't have to hide forever?" he asked, his voice filled with hope.

Omaki smiled. "Not forever, Koda. But for now, we will watch, we will learn, and we will protect our home. And perhaps, one day, we will find a way to live here in peace."

The clans settled into a careful rhythm, watching the homestead from afar and remaining vigilant. They learned to distinguish the family's movements, growing familiar with the boy's routines and the sounds of the animals that lived on the property. They took comfort in the distance, in the quiet respect the humans showed for the land.

With each passing day, the clans grew more at ease, their fears softened by the peace of the forest and the absence of threat. They would remain hidden, but for the first time in memory, they allowed themselves to hope that perhaps, in this place, they had found not only a new sanctuary but a chance at coexistence.

In the evenings, they gathered around Omaki as she told tales of their ancestors, weaving stories of peace and wisdom, reminding them of the strength that came from living in harmony. And as the forest settled into night, they listened to the quiet hum of the homestead nearby, a reminder of the humans who shared their land and of the possibilities that lay ahead.

56

BOND

In the depths of North Carolina's dense woods, the first year the clans spent in their new territory was marked by both wonder and challenge. The clans had chosen this area for its isolation and abundance. Dense forests provided cover and protection, while nearby streams teeming with fish and the surrounding land, rich with berries and edible roots, offered ample sustenance. As they settled into their new home, the clans worked together to strengthen their bonds, sharing knowledge and resources to ensure everyone thrived.

For Koda, the year was particularly transformative. Already standing nearly six feet tall at the age of eight, his massive 13-inch feet left deep impressions in the forest floor, a stark reminder of his unique physicality even among his own kind. Sasquatches, unlike humans, matured quickly in their early years, allowing them to adapt and survive in the wild from a young age. Koda's rapid growth was not just physical. His intellectual and emotional development mirrored his bodily changes. His curiosity about the world was insatiable. He learned quickly, absorbing every lesson the elders taught him about the forest's flora and fauna, the patterns of the weather, and the secrets of the stars that glistened in the clear night skies above their wooded sanctuary.

Koda's curiosity about the boy and his home grew as the months passed, becoming a fascination calling him closer to the world beyond his clan's hidden sanctuary. Koda's young spirit was fueled by wonder, and the boy, Eli, had become an irresistible mystery. To Koda, Eli seemed almost like one of the forest creatures—a curious, friendly soul who offered peace rather than fear, respect rather than hostility.

One evening, when the moonlight cast long shadows over the forest floor, Koda and Paka ventured closer to the homestead than ever before. They remained hidden within the thick woods, their breaths steady as they watched the boy's family finish their meal inside. When the lights dimmed, Eli emerged, holding a bowl of what appeared to be table scraps. He looked toward the woods with a hopeful gaze.

"Here," Eli called softly, his voice barely reaching them through the trees. "This is for you... if you're real. I just want you to know I'm not afraid."

As the boy placed the bowl on a large stump just within the woodbine, Koda felt a surge of warmth. The boy's kindness, so pure and open, was something Koda felt he had to acknowledge. Without hesitation, Koda moved forward, careful to keep low and silent. Paka held back, watching with a mixture of worry and pride. He'd always known Koda's heart was open to all, yet the risks of stepping so close to a human homestead weighed heavily on him.

Koda reached the stump and carefully took the bowl, examining the scraps of food. It wasn't the most appealing offering, and Paka, standing a few paces back, gave a disapproving snort. But to Koda, it was a gesture of friendship, and he eagerly accepted it. Then, remembering Oamki's teachings on respect and reciprocity, he decided to leave something in return.

Earlier that week, Koda had found a bleached white turtle shell by the riverbank, polished by years in the elements until it gleamed under sunlight. To Koda, it felt like a rare treasure, something worth sharing. He placed it gently on the stump, a silent thank-you to the boy whose kindness was as rare as the shell itself.

The next morning, Eli returned to the stump, his face alight with anticipation. When he found the turtle shell in place of the food, his eyes went wide, and a broad grin spread across his face. He picked up the shell, turning it over in his hands as if examining every inch. His imagination was instantly sparked, thoughts swirling about the creatures that might be lurking in the forest, creatures that were not just legends but real, intelligent beings who could understand him.

Eli spent the rest of the day with the turtle shell, showing it to his parents, who indulged him with smiles but dismissed it as a harmless trick of the woods. But to Eli, this was proof—someone, or something, had taken his food and left a gift in return. He felt as if he'd made contact with the forest's mysteries, and he was more determined than ever to strengthen the bond.

Over the coming weeks, the ritual of exchange grew between Koda and Eli. Each time the boy left an offering, Koda would leave something meaningful in return. Sometimes it was a small, intricately woven vine wreath, other times a smooth, polished stone he'd found by the creek. Eli's gifts became more thoughtful, too: fresh apples, honeycomb wrapped in leaves, even a small, hand-painted rock that he'd decorated himself.

For both Koda and Eli, these exchanges were a silent language, a way of saying, "I see you, I understand." Koda felt a kinship with Eli, something deeper than words or boundaries. Paka, ever watchful, remained cautious but respected the boy's innocent attempts to communicate. He saw the way Koda's spirit lifted with each exchange, and though he worried, he understood the value of such a friendship.

As summer turned to fall, the forest became ablaze with colors of orange, red, and yellow, transforming the woodland into a world of warmth and mystery. One evening, as Koda and Paka approached the stump for their usual exchange, they found a small note left beside the offering. Eli had drawn a picture of himself and a figure next to him, a tall creature with large feet, a broad frame, and gentle eyes.

In the drawing, Eli's hand was raised in a wave, and so was the creature's.

Koda felt a strange longing as he looked at the drawing. Though he couldn't read the human writing scrawled next to it, the image spoke volumes. Eli's imagination had taken flight, and he'd now placed Koda in the role of friend, not just a mysterious presence in the woods.

As they watched from the shadows that night, Koda knew their friendship had evolved into something more profound than he could express. Each token they shared, each quiet night spent watching from the woods, was a promise that worlds once divided could bridge their differences through kindness and understanding. And in Koda's heart, a new hope began to grow—that maybe, one day, he and Eli would meet, face to face, under the ancient trees that had borne witness to their silent, wondrous bond.

As their first year in the new home drew to a close, Koda and Eli's friendship had planted seeds of hope and understanding. One crisp autumn day, as leaves painted the ground in hues of fire and gold, Eli ventured closer to the edge of the woods than ever before. Koda, hidden just beyond sight, watched as Eli placed a handcrafted wooden flute on the stump.

"I made this for you," Eli said aloud, his voice carrying a new depth of sincerity. "I hope it reminds you of the wind through the trees, the birds in the morning, and the friendship we share, even if we can't see each other."

Koda stepped out from the shadows, standing tall and proud in the dimming light. Eli, seeing him fully for the first time, wasn't afraid. He smiled, and it was a smile of recognition.

From then on, the stump wasn't just a place of exchange; it was a beacon of unspoken bonds, a testament to the friendship that could exist between two beings from different worlds, united by curiosity, kindness, and a profound respect for the life they shared under the vast, starry sky.

57

REPRIMAND

Asha's voice echoed through the leafy canopy of the dense forest, filled with a mixture of astonishment and concern. "You did what?" she exclaimed, her eyes wide with disbelief as she stared at Koda.

Kabota, standing beside her, added a stern tone to the conversation. "Koda, how could you take such a risk? Showing yourself to the boy—do you understand what this could mean for us all?" The young sasquatch's chest heaved with a mix of fear and defiance. He had never seen his parents this furious. Beside him, Paka stood silent, his gaze lowered, accepting his share of the responsibility.

Omaki, the elder voice of reason, stepped forward, placing a calming hand on Asha's shoulder. "Let's not be too harsh on the boy," she suggested gently. "Yes, he made a mistake, but we must understand why he felt compelled to do this." Koda, gathering his courage, spoke up. "I know it was risky, but Eli—he's different. He understands us, I think. He's never shown any fear, only kindness. I thought..." His voice trailed off under the weight of his parents' stern looks.

Asha sighed, her anger softening a bit as she looked at her son. "Koda, it's not about the boy's character. It's about the safety of our clans. Humans can be unpredictable, and if word spreads about our existence so close to their homes, it could endanger us all."

Kabota nodded, then turned his attention to Paka. "And you, Paka, you've been with him every step of the way. How could you encourage this?"

Paka finally lifted his eyes, his voice steady but filled with regret. "I believed it to be harmless. The exchanges were innocent, and I saw a bond forming that reminded me of the old legends—when humans and sasquatch could share a world in peace. I was wrong to not consider the broader implications."

Omaki, ever the peacemaker, suggested, "Let us not act in haste. We need to observe and see if this interaction leads to any change in human activity around our lands. For now, Koda, you must promise not to seek out the boy again without our consent."

Koda nodded, feeling the weight of his elders' wisdom and his own brashness.

Meanwhile, at the small homestead on the edge of the forest, Eli, bubbling with excitement, rushed into the kitchen where his parents, Thomas and Sarah, were finishing up dinner.

"Mom, Dad, you won't believe it. I saw him—the sasquatch. The one I've been telling you about, the one I've been leaving food for. He's real!" Eli's voice was a mix of excitement and awe.

Thomas, a rugged man with a gentle smile, exchanged a look with Sarah, his eyes twinkling with a mix of skepticism and amusement. "Oh, Eli," Sarah began, her voice filled with the patience of a parent indulging a child's imagination, "we love your stories, but you know, sometimes our minds play tricks on us out there in the woods."

"But it's not just my imagination. I saw him, really. He's tall and covered in hair, and he even left me a painted rock and other gifts before," Eli protested, his young face flushed with the fervor of his conviction.

Thomas chuckled, ruffling his son's hair. "Okay, buddy, maybe it's the same Bigfoot we watch on those reruns of *Finding Bigfoot*, huh? Maybe he came by to say hello."

Sarah smiled, adding, "We've always told you stories about the sasquatches in these woods, haven't we? Let's keep an open mind but remember, it's also important to stay grounded in what we know for sure."

Eli, though slightly disheartened by their disbelief, nodded. He knew what he saw, and he held onto the hope that one day he could prove it to them.

Later that evening, after Eli had gone to bed, Thomas and Sarah sat on their porch, looking out into the starlit woods. "Do you think there's any chance what he's saying could be true?" Sarah whispered.

Thomas took a deep breath, the air filled with the scent of pine and earth. "Maybe," he admitted. "Remember, my grandfather used to talk about seeing them when he was about Eli's age. Who knows? Maybe there's more to this forest than we can see."

They sat together in silence, the night sounds of the forest playing a soft symphony. Inside, the fire of a young boy's conviction burned bright, while outside, the watchful eyes of an ancient clan kept close guard over the unfolding human bonds that tugged at the seams of two worlds.

58

HESITATION

As twilight settled over the Appalachians, the three clans—the Hoh, Riverbend, and Mistwood—gathered in a secluded clearing nestled deep within the dense forest. Shadows stretched long across the ground, and the evening air was thick with anticipation. Over the past few weeks, they had heard strange vocalizations echoing from a distance, deep, resonant sounds that hinted at the presence of other sasquatch clans. The calls were faint but unmistakable, and each member who heard them felt a thrill of cautious hope.

Omaki had called the meeting to discuss their next steps. Tyrek, leader of the Riverbend clan, and Lora, the intuitive and soft-spoken leader of the Mistwood clan, joined her, along with several key members from each clan. Asha and Kabota, ever-vigilant and respected for their wisdom, took seats nearby, listening as the clans' leaders began to speak.

The clearing was silent as Omaki began. "We have all heard the calls," she said, her voice low but clear. "They come at different times —sometimes at dawn, other times at dusk. These sounds, I believe, are more than just the cries of animals. They are the voices of others like us."

The clans listened, nodding in agreement. The vocalizations had been infrequent but distinct, a reminder that the forest around them held more mysteries than they had yet uncovered. Each call, mournful and deliberate, seemed like an attempt to reach out, to connect with anyone who might hear it.

Tyrek shifted, his gaze sweeping over the gathering. "If there is another clan out there, they must be aware of us, just as we are aware of them. I believe they're trying to communicate, to see if we will respond." He paused, looking at Omaki. "The question is... should we?"

There was a sense of agreement, but also tension. Making contact with other clans held the promise of alliances and shared knowledge, but it also carried risks. There was no guarantee that the neighboring clan had the same intentions, and even if they did, any sound loud enough to reach them might also reach the ears of humans.

Omaki glanced at Asha, who sat nearby with her keen eyes fixed on the forest around them. "Asha, you have always understood the old ways. What do you think?"

Asha took a moment before speaking, her gaze distant as she considered her words. "In our ancestors' time, clans were connected, their voices familiar to one another. Calls across the forest were not uncommon, and they helped us share news and form alliances. But times have changed. Humans are more aware now, more attentive. If we answer these calls, we risk exposing ourselves to the homestead family—and perhaps to others."

Her eyes softened as she looked around the clearing. "But there is something else to consider. We left the Olympic Peninsula in search of a new home, and while we have found a place to call our own, it is lonely. Our young ones grow without knowing other clans, without hearing the voices of others like them."

Koda, who sat close to his mother, looked up, his young face full of curiosity. "Are there others like us out there, Mama?"

"Yes, little one. There are others, hidden just as we are. But reaching out is not something we do lightly."

Oamki nodded, adding, "If we choose to respond, it must be with great care, and we must prepare for whatever that response may bring."

Tyrek, ever the pragmatist, leaned forward, his eyes intent as he addressed the clans. "I understand the desire for connection, and I share it. But we must remember why we left our old home. We were not driven out by our own kind, but by humans. And now, here we are, within hearing distance of a human family." He looked at Kabota and Asha, nodding toward the direction of the homestead. "If we are hearing these vocalizations, so are they. And Eli, the boy—he has already sensed our presence, and has seen Koda."

The clans stirred. They knew Eli, the twelve-year-old at the homestead, had shown an unusual sensitivity to the forest. Some of the younger ones had even seen him watching the trees, as though sensing something beyond his understanding.

"If we respond to these calls," Tyrek continued, "it may confirm his parents suspicions. They could begin to connect the dots, perhaps even seek us out. I have no ill will toward this family, but they are humans, and curiosity is their nature. Do we want to invite more attention?"

There was a weight in his words, and the clans grew somber as they considered his perspective. Tyrek's concerns were valid; humans' curiosity had brought them danger before, and there was no guarantee that Eli's family would not react with fear or suspicion if they knew the clans were near.

Lora, the gentle but wise leader of the Mistwood clan, shifted where she sat, her expression thoughtful as she prepared to speak. "Tyrek, I hear you, and I share your caution. But there is also strength in unity. If there is another clan near us, they may have knowledge of this land that we do not. They could warn us of dangers, of human paths, and even help us create a safe haven together."

She paused, looking into the distance, as though sensing the presence of the unknown clan somewhere in the darkening woods. "We left our homes in the Pacific Northwest because we were alone, vulnerable. Here, perhaps we can find strength in numbers."

Omaki nodded, appreciating Lora's perspective. "It is true. With another clan, we could form an alliance, creating a network that spans this land. If humans threaten us, we could stand together."

But the mention of humans brought fresh concern, and Kabota raised a hand to speak.

Kabota, who had spent many nights observing the homestead and keeping the clans hidden from human eyes, was cautious as always. "I understand the value of unity, and I know how powerful it would be to stand together. But if we make contact, we must be prepared to do so quietly, without drawing attention."

His voice grew serious. "Humans are clever. They notice patterns, changes. If we are vocalizing more frequently, they may suspect something. We must assume that Eli's family will hear us, and that they may become more curious than we'd like."

The clans listened in silence, acknowledging the truth in Kabota's words. They had lived as shadows for generations, and any deviation from that could attract attention, even unintentionally. For all the potential benefits of forming an alliance with a nearby clan, they could not afford to be careless.

"I believe we should consider other methods of contact," Kabota continued, his voice thoughtful. "Perhaps, instead of responding with vocalizations, we could leave signs—marks or trails that only another clan would recognize."

The clans nodded in agreement, intrigued. Kabota's suggestion offered a way to communicate without drawing undue attention, and it gave them a measure of control over the situation.

As the discussions continued, Omaki remained quiet, listening to each perspective with respect and consideration. When the clans fell silent, she finally spoke.

"There is wisdom in everything that has been shared tonight," she began. "Tyrek's caution, Lora's belief in unity, Asha's understanding of our heritage, and Kabota's suggestion of subtlety. Each one speaks to our strengths and our hopes." She looked out at the assembled clans.

"I believe that our best path forward is to make contact, but to do so quietly. We can choose a method that allows us to communicate without attracting human attention. As Kabota suggested, signs or marks may be the safest approach."

A quiet approval spread through the gathering, the clans reassured by Omaki's decision. But she was not finished. She looked out into the forest, as though remembering something from long ago.

"Our ancestors knew how to live in harmony with others—both sasquatch and human. They once shared territories, leaving signs to mark boundaries and warn each other of threats. This land may be new to us, but the ways of our people remain. We have the knowledge to live in peace, if we choose to use it."

Omaki went on to share a story from her youth, of a time when her clan had once encountered another sasquatch family. Her elders had marked trees with subtle signs, inviting contact while ensuring that they remained unseen. In time, the two clans had formed a quiet alliance, sharing resources and protection.

The clans listened in rapt silence, Omaki's words painting images of the past that felt both distant and comforting. Her story reminded them of the strength they could find in unity, even if it required patience and caution.

With Omaki's story fresh in their minds, the clans began to discuss the logistics of reaching out to the nearby clan. Kabota suggested marking specific trees along the edges of their territory, using subtle signs that would only be recognized by others of their kind. Lora and Asha agreed to scout the area, identifying paths that might be frequented by the neighboring clan.

The younger members, Koda, Raela, Meika, and Paka, watched with wide eyes as their elders made plans. They could sense the excitement in the air, the promise of connecting with others like themselves. It was a prospect that filled them with both curiosity and a renewed sense of belonging.

As the clans finalized their plans, Tyrek reminded them of the need for caution. "Let us make our intentions clear, but remain wary. If they respond with aggression or disinterest, we will know to leave them be."

Omaki nodded, understanding the importance of Tyrek's words. They would reach out, but they would not force contact. Their approach would be one of patience, guided by the wisdom of their ancestors.

Over the following days, the clans began to mark trees making fresh breaks along the perimeters of their territory, choosing areas that bordered the nearby clan's suspected location. They left subtle signs—scratches on bark, stones arranged in patterns, small branches broken in ways that signified invitation.

Each night, they would gather and listen, waiting for a response. The forest was alive with anticipation, each sound heightened by the hope of connection. The clans shared stories of past encounters, of alliances formed in the old lands, and their voices held a note of optimism that had been absent for so long.

For the young ones, the wait was filled with wonder. Koda, Raela, and Paka would look to the forest with wide eyes, imagining what the neighboring clan might look like, what stories they might bring. The vocalizations from the nearby clan grew stronger, their calls resonant and unmistakable, they sensed the invitation. And each night, as they waited for a response, the clans felt the forest grow smaller, the distances between them diminish, until finally, one evening, a new call echoed through the trees—an answering call, clear and deliberate.

As the answering call drifted through the forest, the clans felt a collective thrill, the realization that their invitation had been heard. They were not alone in this land, and the response was a promise of something greater, something they had longed for since their journey began.

Omaki, Tyrek, and Lora exchanged glances, a silent understanding passing between them. They would approach this new clan with respect, carrying with them the wisdom of their ancestors and the cautious hope of a new beginning. And though the journey ahead remained uncertain, they knew that together, they could face whatever came next.

As they returned to their sanctuary, the clans felt a renewed sense of purpose, a reminder of the strength they held in unity. And as they settled in for the night, the sounds of the forest wrapped around them, no longer distant or unfamiliar, but part of a world where they truly belonged.

59

RESEMBLANCE

The autumn breeze rustled through the trees, carrying the scent of pine and the whispers of turning leaves. Koda, now ten, had grown strong and curious, his steps confident as he explored the familiar paths near the caves. For Koda, these mountains had become his sanctuary, and the voices of the clans—each member a part of his family—filled him with a sense of belonging he had only begun to understand.

As he wandered through the clearing one evening, a new scent drifted on the breeze, a faint but unmistakable trace of something familiar. Koda stopped, his senses attuned, and watched the tree line, sensing that someone was out there, watching.

Days passed, and the signs grew more frequent—unusual calls echoing at dusk, faint but deliberate markings on trees, and shadows that lingered just a moment too long. The clans began to notice, sharing quiet glances and murmurs of curiosity as they recognized the telltale signs of others like them. There was no hostility in the markings, no signs of territorial dispute. If anything, the markings felt like an invitation, a gentle announcement of presence.

Omaki, sensing that the time had come, called a gathering. They would meet the newcomers, but away from the caves, in a place of neutral ground. She sent word to the leaders of each clan, and together they prepared for the meeting.

The clans moved through the forest in near silence, their steps measured, and their eyes sharp as they approached the meeting place. They had chosen a grove of towering oaks, where the branches formed a canopy above and created a sense of privacy and peace. Omaki, Tyrek, Lora, Kabota, and Asha led the gathering, while the younger members, including Koda, stood close behind, their eyes wide with anticipation.

As the clans settled, the newcomers emerged from the shadows. They moved slowly, cautiously, their expressions watchful yet unthreatening. At the front stood a massive male sasquatch, his posture steady and protective. Beside him was a female, her gaze calm and compassionate, and between them, a young female around Koda's age, her eyes bright with curiosity.

The male raised a hand in greeting, his voice a deep rumble. "Thank you for meeting with us," he said, his words carrying the weight of exhaustion and gratitude. "I am Garek, and this is my mate, Raina, and our daughter, Mira. We come from the north, seeking refuge. Our forest... It has been destroyed."

Omaki stepped forward, her voice warm but cautious. "Welcome, Garek, Raina, and Mira. We are sorry for what you have endured. Please, share your story."

Garek exchanged a glance with Raina, his expression somber as he began to speak. "Our territory was once dense, filled with rivers and tall trees. But then the humans came with their machines. They cut down our forest, and with it, they took our home, our food, and our shelter. We tried to remain hidden, to avoid them, but the devastation was too great." He paused, a flicker of pain crossing his face. "We lost members of our clan—some taken by the humans, others lost to starvation. In the end, we had no choice but to leave."

The clans listened, empathy passing through them. They understood all too well the toll human activity could take, the ruthlessness of machines that left no place for creatures of the forest. Koda, standing close to his mother, glanced at Mira, who was watching him with wide, curious eyes. He felt an odd flutter in his chest, a spark of connection that he didn't fully understand but felt drawn to explore.

As Garek and Raina shared more of their story, Koda found himself inching closer to Mira, his curiosity about her growing. He could see the resilience in her gaze, the quiet strength she carried despite the hardships she had faced. Mira, noticing his interest, gave him a shy smile, and soon the two young ones were standing side by side, listening as their elders spoke.

After some time, Omaki motioned for the clans to mingle, allowing everyone to grow comfortable in each other's presence. Koda and Mira took this as their cue, slipping away from the main group and wandering toward a nearby thicket.

"Your home was far away, wasn't it?" Koda asked, his voice filled with wonder as he tried to imagine the forest she had come from.

Mira nodded, her gaze drifting to the treetops. "It was... different. The trees were tall, and the rivers were wide. But it wasn't safe anymore." She looked back at him, a spark in her eyes. "But this place... it feels safe. Do you like it here?"

Koda nodded, a grin spreading across his face. "Yes! I know all the paths, and I can show you the secret streams and the best places to hide. Maybe... Maybe you'll like it here too."

Mira's face softened, and for a moment, they shared a quiet understanding, a connection born of shared experiences and the simple joy of finding a friend.

As the young ones bonded, the elders continued their discussions, weighing the pros and cons of welcoming the new clan fully into their territory. Tyrek, ever cautious, voiced concerns about resources, wondering if they had enough to support the newcomers without straining their supplies. But Omaki, recognizing the strength of unity, argued for inclusion.

"Together, we can watch over more territory, support each other, and face whatever threats come our way," Omaki said. "We have learned that survival comes through strength in numbers. With Garek, Raina, and Mira, we can be stronger."

Lora added her perspective, speaking of the potential for knowledge-sharing. "They may know things about humans, about survival, that we have not yet learned. Their experiences could be invaluable to us."

Finally, after much discussion, the clans agreed to invite Garek's family to join them, to become part of their shared territory, where they could all benefit from each other's strengths.

In the days that followed, Koda and Mira grew inseparable, exploring the forest together and sharing stories. Koda showed her the hidden streams he had discovered, the places where sunlight filtered through the trees in golden beams, and the secret nooks where they could hide from sight. Mira, in turn, taught him the songs of her old forest, the unique calls her clan had used to communicate across distances.

Their friendship blossomed into something deeper, a bond that the elders noticed with a mixture of pride and hope. Asha and Kabota watched them, their hearts swelling as they saw the joy that Mira brought to their son, the way they moved together as though they had known each other all their lives.

As Koda and Mira grew closer, the clans felt the strength of their connection reverberate through the entire community. Their friendship was a reminder of the unity they had sought for so long, the promise of a future built on shared experiences and trust.

With Garek's family now fully integrated, the clans began to operate as a single, cohesive unit. They shared resources, hunted together, and set up patrols along the territory's edges. The forest seemed to embrace the presence of the united clans, its shadows and secrets now a part of their shared world. The sasquatch had found a place where they could not only survive but thrive, a place where they could build a future free from the fear of discovery and the relentless advance of humans.

Koda and Mira, standing at the forefront of this new beginning, embodied the hope of the clans. Their friendship—and perhaps one day, more—was a testament to the resilience of their kind, the strength of unity, and the enduring power of family.

60

POSSIBILITIES

The autumn nights had grown long, filling the forest with a deep, haunting stillness that seemed to amplify the strange sounds drifting through the trees. Eli's parents, Sarah and Thomas, had heard these sounds before—distant howls, guttural calls that echoed off the hillsides. But something about the recent vocalizations felt different, filled with a resonance that set their nerves on edge.

Thomas, a former forest ranger with a wealth of experience tracking local wildlife, usually knew what to expect from the surrounding woods. Coyotes, wolves, even the occasional bear—they were familiar calls, sounds he could identify without a second thought. But these howls, often rising at dusk and continuing through the night, were unfamiliar. They held a rhythm and intensity that suggested intelligence, almost as though something—or someone—was trying to communicate.

One evening, as they sat on the porch listening to the night sounds, Sarah turned to him, a faint worry in her eyes. "Thomas... do you think those are wolves?"

Thomas shook his head, rubbing his chin thoughtfully. "I'm not sure, Sarah. Wolves don't usually stay this close to human territory.

And if they were coyotes, we'd hear the yipping along with it. These sounds... They're different."

Eli, listening from the steps, felt a thrill run through him. To him, it was clear: the howls were from the sasquatch he'd seen last spring. He had never quite gotten over the encounter, and though months had passed, he still looked for signs of his friend whenever he ventured into the woods.

"I think it's the sasquatch," Eli said softly, as though he were sharing a secret.

Thomas and Sarah exchanged a look, each one smiling a little at their son's persistent belief. But they couldn't entirely dismiss it. There was something eerie in the woods that they couldn't explain, and they both felt it.

As the days passed, Sarah and Thomas noticed other things they couldn't easily explain. They'd often walk the property together, checking the pens, tending to their garden, and keeping the perimeter free of debris. On one of these walks, they spotted the first unusual tree break.

A large sapling had been snapped cleanly about six and a half feet above the ground, the splintered wood twisted. Nearby, two smaller branches were arranged in an X, leaning against a rock.

Thomas crouched to examine the break, running his fingers over the jagged wood. "This didn't happen naturally," he said. "It looks deliberate, almost... purposeful."

Sarah studied the tree break. "Could it be some kind of marker? Maybe teenagers messing around?"

Thomas shook his head. "Too high for most kids, and these woods aren't exactly easy to get to. We're miles from the nearest road, and I haven't seen any footprints or signs of human presence."

Eli, who had followed them, looked at the structure with wide eyes. He knew it wasn't made by any human. To him, it looked exactly like the markings he'd read about in books about sasquatches— deliberate communication.

"This is from my friend," Eli said with conviction, his voice brimming with excitement. "He's leaving us signs."

Thomas and Sarah exchanged a glance, each one hesitant to indulge Eli's belief. But the evidence before them was compelling, and neither could shake the feeling that the forest was hiding something extraordinary.

For months, Eli had been leaving small offerings on an old stump at the edge of the forest, hoping his friend would return. The gifting stump, as he called it, had become a ritual, a place where he would leave shiny stones, berries, or small trinkets in hopes that they might be taken in exchange for another encounter. Yet each time he checked, the gifts were left untouched, undisturbed by anything larger than a curious squirrel.

Eli's initial excitement had gradually faded into disappointment. He began to wonder if his friend had moved on, if maybe the sasquatches had left the area in search of more secluded territory. Still, a small part of him held out hope.

One chilly afternoon, Eli sat at the stump with a carefully carved wooden bear. He'd spent days whittling it, smoothing the edges, and giving it life with careful details. He left the carving on the stump, his heart heavy as he whispered, "Please come back. I miss you."

As he walked away, he glanced back one last time, hoping that this time would be different.

Sarah and Thomas's curiosity had grown alongside Eli's, though they kept their suspicions private, not wanting to encourage his sasquatch stories. But the more they observed, the harder it became to explain away the strange occurrences. Unusual calls, tree breaks, X structures—each added a layer to the mystery unfolding around them.

Late one evening, after another round of strange howls, Thomas suggested they set up a trail camera near the gifting stump. "We might catch whoever—or whatever—is out there," he said.

Eli was hesitant at first, fearing the camera might scare his friend away. But when his parents promised to handle the footage with respect and keep an open mind, he agreed, secretly hoping the camera would capture evidence of his friend.

As Thomas secured the camera to a tree, Eli watched with a

mixture of hope and fear, wondering if the sasquatch would avoid the stump entirely. He made a silent wish that the camera would not disrupt the delicate connection he felt with the forest, and more importantly his new friend.

A few days later, Eli returned to the gifting stump, expecting to find his carving untouched. But to his surprise, the carving was gone, replaced by a small bundle of leaves and moss, carefully arranged as though left intentionally. Eli's heart leapt with excitement. He knew this was a sign, a deliberate response from his friend. The bundle, though simple, felt like a message—a connection between two beings from different worlds. He ran back to the house, eager to tell his parents about the exchange.

Sarah and Thomas listened, each feeling a mixture of wonder and caution. Though skeptical, they couldn't deny the significance of the gift Eli had found. Perhaps, they reasoned, something in the forest was watching over their son, connecting with him in ways they couldn't fully understand.

That night, they reviewed the footage from the trail camera, fast-forwarding through images of deer, raccoons, and the occasional fox. But then, near the stump, they saw something strange. A shadowy figure, large and indistinct, appeared at the edge of the frame, lingering for only a moment before disappearing into the trees.

Thomas paused the footage, leaning in closer. Though blurry and barely discernible, the figure's silhouette was unmistakably tall, with a broad, powerful frame.

"That's... not a bear," Sarah whispered.

Eli's face lit up with excitement. "It's him! I knew he was real."

Though still cautious, Sarah and Thomas felt a shift in their perception, the line between reality and mystery blurring as they pondered the existence of Eli's forest friend. They knew, now more than ever, that their homestead was connected to something extraordinary, a force of nature that defied easy explanation.

And as they sat together in the dim light, each lost in their thoughts, they realized that the forest was alive with secrets, its depths more profound and mysterious than they had ever imagined.

61

DELIGHT

Ever since Mira and her family joined the clans, Koda had felt a new thrill running through his days. Mira was a friend, a confidant, and someone who shared his fascination with humans in a way no one else did. Koda had told her about the homestead, about Eli, and the unusual connection he felt to the boy, and Mira had listened intently, her own eyes shining with excitement.

"Koda," she whispered one evening, "do you think we could go see it? The place where he lives?"

Koda's face lit up with a grin. "I was hoping you'd want to. It's not far, and we can stay hidden. I'll show you the stump where we leave gifts for each other."

Mira's smile grew, her curiosity burning brighter than ever. "Let's go," she said, her voice eager but tinged with caution. "I want to see where you've been going all this time."

With the plan made, they set out just before dusk, their steps quiet as they navigated the well-worn paths Koda knew by heart. The forest around them darkened as night fell, casting long shadows that stretched across their path, but Koda felt at ease, his excitement growing with every step.

Koda led the way, moving confidently through the trees, his

senses alert to every sound. He glanced back at Mira, who followed close behind, her eyes wide with wonder as they moved through the forest. Koda could tell that Mira, though used to the wild, found the idea of a human homestead thrilling and strange.

"There's a lot of animals around the house," he whispered as they approached. "Chickens, goats, and even donkeys. They make a lot of noise, but they're harmless."

Mira's eyes lit up at the mention of animals. "I've never seen a donkey before. Or a chicken, for that matter," she admitted. "Only deer and the other creatures that lived near us."

As they got closer, the sounds of the animals reached their ears, a cacophony of clucks, bleats, and the occasional braying. Mira giggled softly, the noise both foreign and amusing to her. Together, they crouched low, moving with caution until the small farmhouse came into view.

Koda pointed toward the edge of the yard, where an old, weathered stump stood near the forest line. "That's the gifting stump," he whispered. "That's where I leave things for Eli, and sometimes he leaves things for me too."

Mira stared at the stump, her curiosity piqued. "It's strange." "We're so different from them, but sometimes... it feels like we're connected, somehow."

Koda nodded in agreement, his eyes on the stump. "I think so too. It's like... some humans understand us better than others." He glanced at Mira, noticing her pensive expression. "Have you ever felt that way? Like you have a connection with them?"

Mira hesitated, then nodded, her eyes filled with a mixture of pride and sadness. "There was a girl... back in my old territory. I saved her life once, and after that, we became friends, in a way."

Koda's eyes widened, his curiosity deepening. "Tell me what happened. I want to hear."

Mira's gaze drifted to the trees, as though she were seeing a memory from long ago. "It was two winters ago," she began. "The days were shorter, and the nights were cold. I was out foraging, looking for anything we could use to get through the season. I was on my way back to our cave when I heard a sound—a small voice, calling for help."

She paused, her expression pained. "It was a little girl, no older than six, I think. She had gotten separated from her parents while they were hiking, and somehow, she'd climbed up into the higher parts of the forest. She was scared, crying for her family... and I couldn't leave her there."

Koda listened, captivated by her story. "What did you do?"

"I picked her up and took her back to our cave," Mira continued. "She was cold and hungry, so I gave her some water and berries. She didn't seem afraid of me, even though she must have known I wasn't human. I stayed with her all night, keeping her warm while the wind howled outside."

"My parents weren't happy about it at first. They were afraid, and thought I'd brought danger to us. But they understood why I did it, and they helped me keep her safe."

Koda's eyes shone with admiration. "You saved her life. That was brave, Mira."

Mira looked down, a small smile on her lips. "The next day, we heard search parties—the humans were looking for her. We could hear helicopters, search planes, and people calling out. My parents helped me sneak her back down to a place near the river, where the searchers would find her."

Koda could see the sadness in Mira's eyes as she remembered. "What happened then?"

"They found her," Mira said. "And after that, I would visit her house from time to time. I'd leave little things by her window, and sometimes she'd leave things for me. It was like... we had a secret friendship, even though we couldn't speak to each other."

Koda felt a deep sense of connection to Mira's story, as though they had both found a part of themselves in the humans they had encountered. It was a feeling of kinship that went beyond words, something powerful and unspoken.

As the two sat in silence by the gifting stump, Mira turned to Koda, her eyes filled with understanding. "Maybe... Maybe there are humans who can understand us, even if they don't know who we are. Maybe that's why we're drawn to them."

Koda nodded, feeling the truth in her words. "Eli feels like that. I think he knows there's more out here than what he's been told." He looked at Mira, his expression thoughtful. "Do you think... we'll always be able to stay hidden?"

Mira's expression grew serious. "I don't know. But maybe we don't have to hide from all of them. Some of them, like your Eli, or the girl I knew... They're different."

They sat together in quiet reflection, each lost in their thoughts. For Koda, the connection with Eli felt like a gift, a reminder that there were beings out there who could see beyond the differences between them. And for Mira, the memory of the little girl she had saved was a reminder that sometimes, in the most unexpected places, kindness could bridge the gap between their worlds.

As the night settled in around them, Koda and Mira made their way back to their families, a new sense of purpose filling their hearts. They would protect their forest, their families, and their secrets. But they would also hold on to the hope that some humans, perhaps a few, could be trusted.

And as they walked through the darkened woods, each step echoing in the quiet night, they felt a newfound sense of unity—a belief that, despite the challenges, there was a place for them in the world, and a future where they could live in harmony with those who shared the land.

62

AWARENESS

The days had grown shorter, the sun casting a softer light over the mountains as the leaves turned vibrant red, orange, and gold. Koda, eleven now, stood taller and moved with a confidence that had grown with each passing season. He felt a strong connection to the forest and his place within the clan, but his visits to the homestead with Mira added a unique thrill to his life, something that felt secret and precious.

Mira, his closest companion, shared his adventurous spirit. They were inseparable, silently exploring and protecting the homestead. Koda knew Mira understood his fascination with Eli's family, having experienced something similar in her old territory. They often discussed it, wondering what drew them to certain humans.

Now, as autumn settled over the land, Koda and Mira found themselves making regular trips to the gifting stump. But over the last few days, the stump had been empty. No shiny stones, no feathers, no small trinkets. Koda felt a strange unease growing within him, his mind drifting to Eli and wondering what had kept him away.

Koda crouched near the stump, his eyes searching the surrounding forest as though expecting Eli to appear at any moment. Mira watched him with concern.

"He hasn't left anything for us in days," Koda said, touching the edge of the stump where he had last placed a gift—a carved piece of wood shaped like a leaf. "It's not like him to just... stop."

Mira, always attuned to Koda's moods, placed a comforting hand on his shoulder. "Maybe he's busy, or maybe he hasn't been able to come out. Sometimes humans get distracted by things we don't understand."

Koda nodded, though his worry didn't ease. The connection he felt to Eli was one of the few constants in his life, something that kept him grounded, even as he embraced his place within the clan. "I know. But... I can't shake the feeling that something's wrong."

After a moment of silence, Mira spoke, her voice firm. "Then let's find out. We can go closer to the house—just once, just to see if he's there."

Koda's eyes brightened at her suggestion. "Are you sure? It could be dangerous."

Mira gave him a confident smile. "I'm with you. And I want to see where he lives."

With that, they made their way through the forest, moving carefully as dusk settled around them, casting the land in shades of deep blue and purple. The homestead lights glowed in the distance, and as they approached, Koda felt a mixture of excitement and trepidation, as they drew closer to Eli's world.

The two young sasquatches moved with practiced stealth, staying low as they approached the homestead. Koda led the way, guiding Mira along the paths he had learned over the past two years of observation.

When they finally reached the edge of the yard, they crouched behind a thick cluster of bushes, their eyes fixed on the house. A warm light glowed from a window, and Koda pointed to it, his voice a whisper.

"There—he's in there. I can feel it."

Mira peered over his shoulder, her eyes wide with wonder. "Do you think he's all right?"

Koda wasn't sure, but something inside him urged him forward. "Let's get closer. Just to see."

They crept across the yard. As they reached the window, they crouched low, peeking inside with a mixture of awe and trepidation.

Inside the cozy living room, Eli sat curled up on the sofa, wrapped in a blanket, his face flushed and eyes drooping. His mother, Sarah, sat beside him, gently brushing his hair back as he coughed, while his father, Thomas, sat next to him with a comforting hand on Eli's shoulder.

Koda and Mira's eyes, however, were drawn to the large glowing box in front of them, an object they had never seen before. Strange images flickered across the screen, lighting up the room with an otherworldly glow. Koda squinted, trying to make sense of what he was seeing.

The images showed humans—men and women dressed in clothes similar to the ones Koda had seen on hikers in the forest. They were speaking to each other in hushed voices, their faces serious as they walked through dense woods, examining trees and markings that looked eerily familiar.

"Look," Mira whispered, her gaze fixed on the screen. "Those markings... They're just like ours."

Koda watched, his unease growing as the humans on the screen pointed out tree breaks, arranged sticks, and rock stacks that matched the communication techniques his clan used. One of the humans made a deep, resonant call, a sound that echoed through the room.

"What are they doing?" Mira asked.

Koda shook his head, unable to look away. "I think... they're looking for us."

The humans on the screen continued their investigation, moving through the forest with a determination that both fascinated and terrified Koda. He watched as they pointed out more signs, speaking of creatures they called "Bigfoot" with a mixture of respect and awe. It was as though they understood something of his world—but without truly knowing it.

"They know we're here," Koda said, the weight of realization settling over him. "They know there are others like us. But they don't really understand."

Mira, equally shaken, placed a hand on Koda's arm, grounding him. "Maybe they're just curious. Like us."

Koda nodded slowly, though a part of him felt exposed, as though his carefully guarded secret had been laid bare. Yet there was also a strange sense of connection. If these humans on the screen were searching for sasquatches, maybe they weren't so different after all.

As they watched, Mira noticed that Eli seemed tired, his face pale as he leaned against his mother. She pointed to him, concern in her eyes. "I think he's sick, Koda. That's why he hasn't come to the stump."

Koda felt worry, his initial excitement replaced by sympathy for his friend. He wanted to do something, to help Eli as Mira had once helped the girl she had saved. But he knew getting too close would be dangerous, both for him and for his family.

"We should go," Mira whispered, sensing his conflict. "He'll be all right. Humans have ways of healing."

Reluctantly, Koda nodded, taking one last look at Eli before he and Mira slipped back into the shadows, their steps silent as they retreated to the forest.

As they made their way back through the trees, Koda and Mira talked about what they had seen, their voices hushed.

"They're trying to understand us," Koda said. "But they don't know the whole truth."

Mira nodded, her expression thoughtful. "Maybe that's a good thing. If they knew too much, they might not leave us alone."

When they reached the clan, Koda shared their discovery with Omaki, Kabota, and the others. The elders listened intently, exchanging concerned glances as they absorbed the implications of the humans' knowledge.

"It seems humans are more aware than we thought," Omaki said, her tone serious. "We must be cautious. They may not know everything, but they are watching."

Asha nodded, her gaze thoughtful. "Perhaps this will remind us to guard our secrets carefully. Curiosity can be a dangerous thing."

But despite the warnings, Koda couldn't shake the feeling that he and Eli shared a connection deeper than mere curiosity. He knew he would continue his visits to the stump, hoping that one day, Eli would be there waiting, ready to share in the silent understanding that had brought them together.

And as the clans settled for the night, the forest wrapped around them, a veil of mystery and protection, hiding secrets that, for now, would remain safely in the shadows.

Koda had returned to the forest that night with more questions than he had ever known possible. For days, he replayed the scene he and Mira had witnessed through the homestead window: Eli's family watching a glowing box filled with images of humans dressed in forest clothing, imitating the calls and signs that his own clan used to communicate. The sight of those humans had unnerved him, stirring memories he had tried to keep buried.

He couldn't shake the feeling that there was something he needed to understand, something only Eli could help him figure out. Why were these humans searching? What were they looking for? And if they found it... What would they do?

Mira noticed his restlessness. They had spent almost every day together since they first met, and she could read him better than anyone. "You haven't been yourself since we went to the homestead," she said one evening, her eyes studying him with quiet concern. "You've got questions. More than usual."

Koda sighed, glancing at the forest stretching out before them. "I do. Seeing those humans, the ones looking for us... it reminded me of the ones who attacked our clan before, back in the Olympic Peninsula. But Eli and his family... they don't seem the same. I don't know if they're a danger or... just curious."

Mira nodded thoughtfully. "Humans can be strange. Some of them can be so destructive, and yet, some seem so gentle, like Eli. But if you want answers, it could mean putting yourself at risk. Have you thought about what you'll do?"

Koda hesitated, his gaze distant. "I don't know yet. But I have to understand. I can't shake the feeling that there's something important I need to know."

The next day, Koda confided more in Mira, voicing his fear that the humans' curiosity could lead them to harm the clans. "If they're anything like the humans who raided our home before, they won't stop until they find us."

Mira's eyes softened. "I know it's important to you, Koda. But think carefully. Eli might be kind, but his family... and the others... they could bring more humans if they start to believe we're really out here. What happens if Eli can't keep our secret?"

Koda nodded slowly, her words echoing his own worries. "You're right, Mira. But maybe... Maybe if I could just talk to him, just this once. Then I could understand what humans like him are truly after."

"If you go, just... be careful, Koda. The forest depends on us staying hidden, and our family needs you safe."

Koda gave her a smile, though his mind was still clouded with uncertainty. "I'll be careful, Mira. I promise."

The memories of the Olympic Peninsula, though distant, came rushing back to Koda in vivid detail. He remembered the day the humans had come, their machines tearing through the forest, their voices loud and harsh as they drove the clans out. He could still feel the terror, the cries of those caught off guard, and the pain of leaving behind the only home they had ever known.

But here, in these new mountains, things felt different. Eli's family wasn't the same as the humans who had brought harm to his clan. They lived quietly, seemed to respect the forest in their own way, and had shown kindness through the small gifts left on the stump.

And yet, the humans on the screen troubled him. He couldn't help but wonder if their curiosity could eventually lead them to his clan. This question, more than anything else, prompted him to seek answers.

63

KINSHIP

In the days that followed, Koda lingered near the stump, staring into the trees, lost in thought. The idea of showing himself to Eli again seemed reckless and bold, yet the thought filled him with a strange sense of purpose. He thought about the last time he had seen Eli, how the boy had watched the forest with a look of quiet wonder, as though he could sense Koda's presence without truly knowing it.

Mira's words echoed in his mind, urging caution. He knew that she feared for his safety, and he didn't want to risk the clan's secrecy. But the need for answers outweighed his fears. He thought of leaving a sign, something unmistakable that would bring Eli to the stump, but even that felt insufficient. He wanted to speak to Eli, to make him understand the importance of the forest and the clans that lived within it.

Could he make Eli understand? Could they find a way to communicate, despite their differences?

Koda spent hours alone, hidden in the shadows of the trees, weighing the risks and imagining the possible outcomes. What if Eli didn't understand? What if, by showing himself, he exposed the clan to danger? Although he was deeply afraid of the unknown, the thought of doing nothing, of leaving these questions unanswered, was unbearable.

He had seen the bond between his family and the forest, the way each member worked to protect their world. And perhaps, he thought, Eli could be a part of that bond. The boy already showed signs of understanding, of kindness. Maybe, if he tried, Koda could help Eli see the truth.

But if he was wrong, the consequences could be severe.

After days of quiet reflection, Koda finally made his decision. He would go to the stump that night, wait for Eli, and reveal himself. Just once. Just to ask his questions.

As the sun set over the mountains, Koda felt a mix of excitement and nervous energy. He had spent the day preparing himself, running over the questions he would ask, imagining Eli's reaction. He was aware that Mira would be eagerly waiting for his return, and he made a mental commitment to exercise caution and avoid taking unnecessary risks.

As the forest darkened, Koda moved through the trees, his steps quiet and purposeful. He reached the edge of the clearing where the stump stood, bathed in moonlight, and settled into the shadows to wait. The forest around him was alive with nocturnal sounds—the hoot of an owl, the rustling of leaves, the distant call of coyotes—but his focus remained on the path from the homestead.

He didn't know how long he waited, but finally, he saw movement. Eli, wrapped in a warm coat, was walking slowly toward the stump, his gaze scanning the trees with an expression of quiet hope.

Koda's heart pounded as he stepped forward, his form emerging from the shadows. He watched as Eli froze, his eyes widening in awe and disbelief. For a moment, neither of them moved, each one staring at the other with a mixture of fear and wonder.

Then, with a deep breath, Koda took a step closer, raising his hand in a gesture of peace. Eli's face softened, and slowly, he took a step forward as well.

Koda felt a wave of relief and anticipation. The moment he had dreamed of was here, and now, he had a chance to find the answers he needed. He met Eli's gaze, his mind filled with questions, and hoped that, somehow, they would find a way to understand each other.

Koda stepped forward, emerging from the shadows with slow, measured steps. Eli stood a short distance away, frozen in place, his eyes wide as he took in the sight of Koda. The boy's face was a mixture of awe and fear, his mouth slightly open as though he wanted to speak but couldn't find the words.

Koda, feeling a surge of courage, took another step closer, raising one hand in a gesture of peace. He wanted to communicate, to break the silent barrier between them. But before he could, a distant voice called out from the homestead, shattering the stillness.

"Eli! Supper's ready!" The voice was warm and gentle, but to Koda, it was a warning. His muscles tensed as instinct took over, and he dropped to all fours, the urge to flee overpowering his curiosity.

Eli turned, glancing back toward the house, a look of frustration and reluctance on his face. When he turned back to look at Koda, the space where Koda had stood was empty. Koda had vanished, already halfway into the cover of the forest.

Koda moved swiftly through the trees, the sound of his own breathing loud in his ears. He didn't stop until he was deep within the forest, the soft rustle of leaves around him a reassuring presence. Slowly, he stood up, his heart still pounding as he replayed the moment in his mind.

Part of him felt disappointed, the abrupt end to their encounter leaving a lingering ache. He had come so close to breaking through, to understanding what Eli knew. But fear—instinctual and immediate—had driven him away, reminding him of the danger in drawing too close to the human world.

Yet the thrill of that brief connection remained, urging him to go further, to try again. Koda took a deep breath, gathering his thoughts as he began the journey back to the cave, already planning his next move.

64

CONNECTION

When Koda reached the cave, Mira was there, her face lighting up when she saw him. "Did you see him?" she asked, her voice filled with excitement and curiosity.

Koda nodded, his eyes shining as he relayed the details of their encounter. "I was so close, Mira. He looked... surprised, but not afraid. I think he wanted to talk."

Mira listened, her face thoughtful. "But you left?"

Koda sighed, rubbing the back of his neck. "His mother called for him, and it... startled me. I ran before he could get close. But... I can't stop thinking about it, Mira. I want to know more."

"I understand, Koda. But be careful. Humans... They're not always like Eli. We can't risk drawing attention to ourselves."

Koda nodded, though her words didn't quiet his desire for answers. He knew she was right, but he also felt that the questions weighing on him couldn't be left unanswered.

Over the next few days, Koda kept returning to the memory of their encounter—of Eli standing there, his face filled with awe. The questions lingered, growing louder in his mind until he could no longer ignore them. Finally, he decided to seek out Omaki, hoping her wisdom would help him find a path forward.

One evening, as the sun dipped below the horizon, Koda approached Omaki, finding her alone as she watched the forest. She looked up as he approached, a soft smile on her face.

"Omaki," he began, hesitant. "There's something I need to ask you."

She nodded, her expression patient and open. "What is it, Koda? You look troubled."

Taking a deep breath, Koda explained his encounter with Eli, his desire for answers, and the questions that had been growing in his mind since that night. Omaki listened intently, her face thoughtful as she absorbed his words.

When he finished, Omaki sat in silence for a moment, her gaze distant as though lost in memory. Finally, she spoke, her voice low and filled with the weight of history.

"Long ago, Koda, our kind lived close to the Native American tribes. We shared the forests, and in time, we learned to communicate with them. They respected us, and we respected them. They knew we were part of the land, and they treated us with honor."

She paused, her expression softening as she continued. "When the white men came, we learned some of their language too, blending it with what we knew from the tribes. It became a way for us to understand each other, to share the forest without fear."

Koda listened, his eyes wide. He had always known the sasquatch clans communicated, but he hadn't realized they had once spoken to humans as well.

"So... if I were to speak to Eli," he began slowly, "he might understand me?"

Omaki nodded. "If you use the old words, he should. But remember, Koda, communication is a gift. We do not share it lightly. Our history with humans is complicated, and we must be careful who we trust." Koda felt a sense of awe and gratitude, understanding the depth of the knowledge Omaki had shared. He realized that his desire for answers was part of something much larger, a legacy passed down through generations.

Omaki looked him in the eye, her gaze steady and serious. "If you choose to speak to Eli, Koda, be wise. Humans can be both kind and dangerous. Choose your words carefully, and do not reveal more than necessary."

"I understand your need for answers, but remember that some things are better left unknown. Our secrets keep us safe, and safety must always come first."

Koda nodded, feeling the weight of her words. "Thank you, Omaki. I'll be careful. I just... I need to know."

Omaki smiled, her face filled with warmth. "I know, Koda. Curiosity is a powerful thing, but so is caution. Go with a clear mind and open eyes, and trust yourself."

With Omaki's blessing and guidance, Koda felt a new sense of purpose. He would approach Eli once more, this time armed with the wisdom of his ancestors and the knowledge that, if he chose his words carefully, he might finally bridge the gap between their worlds.

The sun had descended below the horizon, casting a cool, shadowed blue hue over the forest. Koda took a deep breath, his heart pounding with excitement as he prepared for his second attempt to meet Eli. This time, he felt more prepared, more confident in his abilities. Omaki's tales of the ancient ways had instilled in him a sense of assurance, reminding him that he was not the first of his kind to bridge the gap between their worlds. As he slipped through the trees, the crisp night air felt invigorating, a stark contrast to the approaching winter. The brittle leaves and the whispers of frost on the ground signaled the season's change. Reaching the wood line near the homestead, Koda settled into a secluded spot, his gaze fixed on the small house.

He knew Eli's routine well, had watched as the boy went about his evening chores. Soon enough, he saw Eli stepping out, bundled in a thick coat, his face lit by the faint glow from the homestead's windows. Koda took a steadying breath, waiting until Eli moved toward the fenced area with the animals.

With a soft, distinct whistle, Koda called out, careful to keep his voice low.

Eli's head turned, his eyes searching the dark edges of the trees.

He took a tentative step forward, his face breaking into a cautious but excited smile as he spotted Koda's silhouette.

Koda stepped forward just enough to be visible, watching as Eli approached, his steps slow and respectful. They met just inside the wood line, the space between them filled with unspoken wonder. Eli, though wide-eyed, seemed calm, his curiosity outweighing any fear.

"Hi," Eli whispered. "I knew... I knew you were real."

Koda nodded, his gaze steady. He felt a strange sense of familiarity with Eli, a feeling that transcended the differences between them. "You... You left gifts," Koda said slowly, using simple English, just as Omaki had instructed.

Eli's face brightened. "You saw them? I didn't know if you'd take them."

Koda nodded again, feeling a warmth that he hadn't expected. For the first time, he felt understood, as though he had found a connection that bridged the gap between their worlds.

Eli's excitement was palpable as he took another small step forward, his voice filled with wonder. "I've been waiting for so long... I wanted to meet you. My name is Eli. Can you... can you understand me?"

Koda nodded, his voice low but clear. "Koda. My name is Koda."

The two stared at each other in the quiet, each feeling the weight of the moment. For Koda, it was as if the world had narrowed to just this small space between them, a place where fear and curiosity blended together.

Remembering Omaki's advice, Koda took a deep breath, summoning the courage to ask the questions that had been haunting him. "The box... I saw humans. In the forest... looking. Why?"

Eli's face softened in understanding. "You mean the television?" He glanced back at the homestead, a faint smile on his lips. "That was a show called 'Finding Bigfoot.' It's about people trying to learn about sasquatches. They're not looking to hurt you. They want to prove you exist, to show everyone that you're real."

. . .

Koda listened carefully, processing Eli's words. The idea of humans actively searching for his kind, not out of malice but out of curiosity, was strange and unsettling. "They... They don't want to harm?"

Eli shook his head firmly. "No. My family watches the show because we think you're amazing. We don't want to hurt you, Koda. We just... We just want to know more."

Koda felt a weight lift from his heart, though caution lingered. Humans wanted to understand, not harm. It was a strange comfort, one that filled him with both hope and unease.

Eli looked around, his voice dropping to a whisper. "My mom and dad... they heard some of your calls. They put up a trail camera to see if we could see you."

Koda's heart fluttered, a flicker of fear flashing through him. "They... saw me?"

Eli nodded, his expression serious. "Just a glimpse. They didn't tell anyone, though. They don't want people coming here and bothering you."

Koda felt a mix of gratitude and caution. Eli's family had kept their secret, but the fact that they had captured his image made him realize just how close he had come to exposure. Their conversation was suddenly interrupted by a long, mournful howl echoing through the forest. It was unlike any sound Koda had heard before—low, eerie, and filled with intensity.

Koda's body tensed, his instincts on high alert. He didn't recognized the sound, but it didn't sound good. Eli, too, looked startled, glancing into the shadows as though he could see the source of the noise.

"What... What is that?" Eli whispered, his voice shaking.

Koda shook his head, his eyes filled with warning. "Not safe."

At that moment, Eli's father, Thomas, stepped outside, his voice breaking the silence. "Eli! Time to come in, buddy."

The boy looked back at Koda, his expression filled with reluctance and worry. "I have to go," he said softly. "But... will you come back?"

Koda nodded, his eyes solemn. "I'll return. Be... careful."

With one last look, Eli turned and ran back to the homestead, leaving Koda alone in the growing darkness. He waited until the boy was safely inside, then slipped back into the forest, the sound of the howl still echoing in his mind.

When Koda returned to the cave, he found the clans gathered, their faces tense as they discussed the night's events. The strange howl had reached their ears, and the air was thick with apprehension.

Omaki, Tyrek, and Lora stood at the center of the meadow, their expressions serious as they addressed the clans. "That howl," Tyrek began, his voice low, "belongs to Dogmen. They are known for their aggression and disregard for secrecy."

Lora nodded, her face filled with concern. "They don't follow the old ways. They see humans as intruders and threats, and they won't hesitate to strike out if they feel challenged."

Omaki looked at Koda, her eyes filled with understanding. "This is why we have been cautious, Koda. Not all of our kind share our respect for the balance of the forest. The Dogmen are dangerous, and if they draw the attention of humans, it could put us all at risk."

Koda listened, a sense of dread settling over him. The encounter with Eli had brought him answers, but it had also reminded him of the dangers that lay beyond the safety of their territory. He glanced back toward the homestead, his heart heavy with the knowledge that Eli, too, could be caught in the crossfire if the Dogmen grew too bold.

As the clans continued to engage in quiet conversation, Koda was determined to remain vigilant. He would protect the secret of their existence, not only for his family but for the boy who had shown him a glimpse of the human world. And as the night deepened, he knew his journey was far from over—both in understanding the humans and in guarding against the dangers that lurked within his own kind.

EPILOGUE

Eli slipped inside, his mind still buzzing from his brief but thrilling encounter with Koda. The strange howl had left him shaken, a reminder of the dangers that lurked in the woods beyond the warmth of his home. His father looked up from the living room, his expression a mix of concern and curiosity.

"Did you hear that, bud?" Thomas asked, his voice serious. "That howl... It sounded massive. Almost like a wolf, but different."

Eli nodded, glancing back toward the door, half-expecting to hear the eerie sound again. "Yeah, I heard it. It was... strange."

Sarah joined them, her eyes full of worry. "Are you sure you're all right, Eli? I didn't like the sound of that howl at all. It seemed... too close."

Eli nodded, feeling a warmth at his family's concern. "I'm okay, Mom. Just... curious about what it was."

Thomas, picking up on the tension, tried to lighten the mood with a grin. "Well, maybe it was a Dogman. We just listened to that story about Dogmen on 'Sasquatch Odyssey,' remember?"

Eli's eyes widened, intrigued. "Dogman? Like... a big wolf that stands up, like Koda?"

Thomas nodded, chuckling. "Yep. Folks say it's like a werewolf— massive, upright, with glowing eyes. Supposedly, it's a rival to the sasquatches. Old stories say that Dogmen and sasquatches don't get along."

Eli's curiosity flared, mingling with the thrill and apprehension still lingering from the night's events. "So, it's real?" he asked.

Thomas shrugged, a smile tugging at the corner of his mouth. "Well, I don't know. But some people think so. There are stories of Dogmen sightings, especially in areas where sasquatch sightings happen. They say Dogmen and sasquatches used to fight over territory. And if those stories are true... they're not exactly friendly."

Sarah gave a small, skeptical laugh, but Eli could see a hint of fascination in her eyes. "I never thought I'd be talking about Dogmen and sasquatches at the same time," she said, "but after some of the things we've heard around here... I guess anything's possible."

Eli's heart pounded with excitement. The idea of creatures like

Koda and something even more fearsome prowling the same forest filled him with a strange exhilaration. "Maybe it was a Dogman," he said softly, glancing out the window. "Maybe they're closer than we think."

As they settled into the living room, Eli peppered his dad with questions, eager to hear more about the Dogmen. Thomas, warming to the topic, recounted some of the stories he had heard on their favorite podcast.

"There are legends from all over about them," he explained, his voice low and mysterious. "People say Dogmen have been around as long as sasquatches, maybe longer. They're fierce and don't like sharing their space. There are tales of Dogmen ambushing hikers and chasing them out of the woods.

Eli's mind whirled, a mixture of excitement and apprehension filling him. Could Koda know about the Dogmen? Did he understand the danger they posed?

Sarah looked at her son, her eyes softening. "Just be careful, Eli. Whatever's out there, we don't know if it's friendly."

Eli nodded, though his mind was already racing with plans. The strange howl and the stories of Dogmen were more than just spooky tales to him—they were mysteries, questions that needed answers. And he knew that Koda might hold the key.

Back in the caves, the sasquatch clans were gathered in anxious conversation, the echoes of the strange howl still fresh in their minds. The elders sat at the center, their faces solemn as the younger members crowded around, eager for answers.

Tyrek, his gaze dark and serious, began to speak, his voice carrying the weight of ancient knowledge. "What we heard tonight was no ordinary wolf. That howl belongs to the Dogmen—a breed that shares our forests but not our ways."

The younger sasquatch listened, their eyes wide. Koda, still shaken from his encounter with Eli, leaned forward, absorbing every word.

"The Dogmen are fierce and territorial," Tyrek continued. "They roam in packs, and they do not respect the ways of peace. They have clashed with our kind for centuries, driven by hunger and aggression. If they are near, we must be on guard."

Omaki, who had listened quietly, added her own wisdom to Tyrek's words. "The Dogmen once formed alliances with humans, using their strength and cunning to hunt us. They understand the language of both beast and man, and they do not forgive easily. If they are in our territory, it could mean they are seeking revenge or reclaiming old grounds."

The clan fell silent, each one processing Omaki's words. The Dogmen were more than just creatures—they were a threat that could not be ignored. Koda glanced around, noting the expressions of unease on the faces of his friends and family.

Omaki's eyes met his, her gaze filled with both understanding and caution. "Koda, you have seen much of the human world. But remember that even among creatures like us, there are those who cannot be reasoned with. If the Dogmen are close, you must be vigilant. They are as clever as they are dangerous."

Koda nodded, feeling the weight of her warning. His recent encounters with Eli had stirred his curiosity, but the presence of the Dogmen introduced a new layer of risk, one that could endanger not only himself but his entire clan.

With Tyrek and Omaki's stories fresh in their minds, the clan leaders began organizing a plan to protect their territory. Tyrek suggested setting up patrols along the borders, and Omaki proposed an early-warning system to alert the clans of any approaching threat.

The younger members of the clan, including Koda and Mira, listened eagerly as the elders outlined their strategy. They learned the signals used by their ancestors to communicate across distances, the subtle calls and gestures that would keep them hidden while allowing them to warn each other of any danger.

Koda felt a renewed sense of responsibility, his mind racing with both excitement and apprehension. The threat of the Dogmen loomed large, a reminder of the delicate balance that existed between the sasquatch and the world around them.

As the clan settled in for the night, the stories of ancient conflicts and the howl of the Dogmen echoed in Koda's mind. He knew that the days ahead would require caution, courage, and perhaps more trust than he had ever dared to give. And as he lay in the quiet of the cave, he couldn't help but wonder what his next meeting with Eli might reveal—and if their fragile friendship would be enough to withstand the dangers closing in around them.

ABOUT THE AUTHOR

Brian, a native of Northwestern Georgia, has been captivated by the mysteries beyond our understanding since childhood. Enthralled by tales of hairy creatures in the mountains near his home, a personal encounter as a child ignited his deep fascination with Sasquatch, propelling him into a world of endless exploration.

After a sixteen-year career in law enforcement, Brian turned his passion into a hobby by starting a podcast. Unexpectedly, this hobby evolved into something much greater. By 2022, his *Sasquatch Odyssey* podcast had become one of the most popular shows in the realm of Sasquatch encounters, captivating a diverse audience. Brian has conducted hundreds of interviews with eyewitnesses and undertaken field research on his expansive forty-acre property in North Carolina, as well as in Tennessee and British Columbia, Canada—all in pursuit of answers to the Sasquatch mystery.

Brian's success and his knack for captivating storytelling have earned him recognition beyond the podcasting world. He has been a guest on numerous podcasts and featured on television shows aired on the Vice Network and Tubi. As a skilled public speaker and host, he has graced the stages of Sasquatch conferences and festivals across the United States and around the world.

Not content with a single venture, Brian is also the founder and CEO of Paranormal World Productions, LLC. In addition to *Sasquatch Odyssey*, he hosts other intriguing podcasts such as *The Guilty Files*, *Backwoods Bigfoot Stories*, *Weird Encounters*, and *That Bigfoot Podcast*, showcasing his diverse talents and unwavering commitment to exploring the uncharted territories of the paranormal world.

ALSO BY BRIAN KING-SHARP

Sasquatch Unleashed: The Truth Behind the Legend

AFTERWORD

Go to hangarıpublishing.com to learn more about the Authors and stay up to date with their newest releases.